Introduction to the A.R.T. System

By Rory Feeney

Contents

iii

Foreword

This book was originally written as a set of modules to accompany a course composed of eight sections; it was then edited to serve as a guide for tutors and course leaders and is now being made available to experienced and novice actors as an introduction to the A.R.T. system.

Although it is divided into chapters, these sections would best be viewed as modules to be worked on using the exercises provided, and the concepts applied to text and improvised situations, before moving on to the next section. To aid the reader's understanding, important words and concepts are capitalised. For the experienced actor or course leader it may be read from cover to cover in one sitting and be clearly understood, but it is intended to accompany a steady process of application and development.

There are many different approaches to actor training. Few if any are regarded as complete and nearly all contain conflicts with other systems.

Within each school of thought there are differing degrees of haziness or lack of precision, which can lead even the most diligent student to feel lost or at best unclear on how to apply the ideas presented.

The A.R.T. System is an attempt to formulate a clear and precise framework for dealing with many of the fundamental parameters that exist within the wide field of actor training. It is by no means intended to be complete as it merely touches on the parameters of movement and voice, doesn't mention previous circumstances or a character's past life and makes no attempt to cover the complex area of character development.

What this book does attempt to do is to open the door to clear and precise control of many aspects of an actor's range and allow dynamic control of the parameters of drama within scenes. Although its application will be useful in improvised work, the primary intention for its use is acting with dialogue.

Excerpts from *A Doll's House* by Henrik Ibsen are reproduced with the kind permission of Project Gutenberg.

Introduction

Acting is often described as an art, sometimes a craft and very occasionally a science. This may be because the skills or tools required to be a good actor are extremely varied and as a complete set are very difficult, if not impossible, to list or define. While there are elements in which certainty can be found, much of the terrain that actor and director negotiate is hazy and vague.

The A.R.T. System is an attempt to clearly define parameters which will accurately describe and control the many intangible forces at play within human interaction. The mechanisms used are directly based on what actually happens in real life, and as a consequence the results attain new levels of naturalism.

This is a nuts-and-bolts system, and actors working with the system will train each parameter separately, learning how to manipulate dynamics clearly and efficiently. Once rudimentary training has been covered, the actor will be able to make small and precise changes which will in turn produce startlingly powerful effects.

Although the A.R.T. System initially seems to be highly technical in nature, well-trained actors who have been introduced to the system have praised the freedom and clarity which it allows. As with many detailed approaches to all sorts of skills, the learner must fully embrace basic training before they can harvest the fruits of their early labour.

Chapter 1: Playing Objectives

All dialogue can be linked to at least one Objective, in that the speaker is using words in an attempt to achieve something, primarily from the person or persons being addressed.

Humans developed speech as a means to help satisfy needs, and these needs will differ greatly in their level of importance and urgency. A need for food may be ranked higher than a need for love, and a need for love may rank higher than a need for reassurance. Sometimes the Objective will be explicitly stated in the line, but often there will be other Objectives being pursued.

One of the simplest and most common phrases is 'Hello', but what might the Objective be? At first one might decide that it is 'to let the other person know I'm here', but unless they can't see or hear you, the Objective must be something more than simply alerting them to your presence.

If there's a possibility that they don't know you're there (perhaps you've entered a shop and it appears to be empty), then your Objective may be 'to let the other person know that I'm not a thief' or 'to reassure the other person that I'm polite, friendly and honest'. If you compare these two Objectives you may conclude that the second encompasses the first, i.e. a thief is not usually deemed to be polite, friendly and honest. In fact, in this kind of situation the Objective will actually cover more than this, as we shall see.

What will determine whether we say hello to somebody or not? It will usually be because we already have, or we expect to have, some kind of relationship with that person.

The best way to discover the Objective is to ask 'What Response do I want from the person I'm talking to?' With a greeting such as 'Hello' we usually want the other person to acknowledge our presence, or our worth and value, either generally or in the context of that specific location, so the person may nod or smile and offer a similar greeting.

If we look at unsatisfactory Responses they will usually be the opposite of this: a look of disapproval or unfriendliness, or perhaps even a Response such as 'What are you doing here?', will usually be unsatisfactory.

By looking at unsatisfactory outcomes we will often discover that the Objective is the opposite of that outcome. A good way to discover an obscure Objective is to imagine the worst outcome and then determine the exact opposite. For example, the worst outcome from the phrase 'I like your new hat' may be a Response such as 'I don't care what you think!'; this suggests that the Objective may be the opposite, something like 'to get the other person to acknowledge the value of my opinion' or, if the speaker is relatively unacquainted with the person, 'to make the other person see the value of becoming my friend'.

So we can see that the Objective of a greeting such as 'Hello' will often be something like 'to make the other person acknowledge the value of my presence'.

This will of course vary according to character and situation.

The Objective of saying 'Hello' at a job interview might be 'to make the other person see me as a confident and friendly person'.

The Objective of saying 'Hello' upon entering a shop might be 'to gain the full and willing attention of the shopkeeper'.

The Objective of saying 'Hello' when challenged by a security guard might be 'to make the security guard see me as an unthreatening person'.

We can see that the above examples are all more specific versions of 'to make the other person acknowledge the value of my presence'.

A greeting such as 'Hello' can actually be used in an unfriendly way, for example to make somebody go away; this will be covered when we deal with *Transitive Verbs*.

Now let's consider the line 'May I have a drink of water?' The obvious Objective will be that the speaker (person A) needs water, but is this all they need? If the person they are speaking to (person B) gives them a glass of water accompanied by an unfriendly look then the speaker may be left feeling unsatisfied. This implies that being given water alone is only part of A's Objective.

The best possible outcome may be that B responds by saying 'Certainly. Is there anything else I can do for you?' As long as this is said with sincerity, A will probably be satisfied.

So there are two levels to the Objectives in this example: one is explicitly stated in the line and is usually of a somewhat practical nature, and the other, which is not stated in the line, is of a more personal or psychological nature.

We might describe the Objective as 'to get water while being treated with kindness and respect'.

But surely everyone wants to be treated with kindness and respect? Well, although most people do, the importance of this varies enormously depending on the individual. To some it is vital that they are treated with kindness and respect, and these people will be more sensitive to the behaviour of others; to other people it may not be of such importance. Someone who feels particularly under-valued may have a greater need to be treated with respect and kindness; someone with high self-esteem may not have as much need to be treated this way. This shows how a character's personal needs will be represented along with their practical needs when defining their Objectives.

Now consider the line 'Who cut your hair?', spoken by A to B. Although the Objective initially appears to be 'to discover who has cut B's hair' there is obviously something more going on. One choice may be that A dislikes the haircut and is mocking B; another choice may be that A is very impressed with the haircut and is flattering B. Either of these choices will be reasonable and may be delivered truthfully, but to simply choose the Objective explicitly stated in the line (to discover who has cut B's hair) will lead to a dull, robotic and untruthful delivery of the line.

Let's consider what the Objective might be in the scenario where A uses the question to mock B? To answer this accurately we need to know more about their relationship. If we don't know anything more than what is contained in the line then we need to make some choices.

Mockery will usually take one of two forms: light-hearted and gentle mockery or vindictive and bullying mockery. Let's choose the light-hearted mockery. In this scenario, A may be teasing B by making them think that their hair looks bad before telling them that it actually looks good. The difficulty for A will be that, if they have this kind of relationship, B will probably know that A is only teasing. Consequently, A will have an idea of how they want B to react to the line. For example, A may want to see a genuine expression of shock or concern on B's face. Making specific choices such as these will help to define a character's Objective more precisely.

By defining the Objective in terms of 'what I want the other person to *DO* or *SAY*', the Objective will always aim to initiate a specific Response from the other character or characters.

This in turn will focus the actor on affecting the other people in the scene and will take the actor's focus away from themselves, thereby helping to solve the problem so common in the development of a novice actor: self-consciousness. This reduction in self-awareness allows the voice and body to operate without the actor's direct attention, producing more naturalistic behaviour.

The importance of defining the Objective in terms of 'what I want the other person to *DO* or *SAY*' can be clearly seen if we look at an argument. Let's imagine two people who disagree so strongly that they are arguing. Their dialogue will be energetic and could last for hours without being resolved; it may even continue months later when they next meet. If you ask each of them 'What could the other person *DO* or *SAY* to completely stop the argument?' you will discover their Objective, and a little more interrogation will define it very precisely.

A might say 'If B were to apologise the argument would end' and B might say 'If A admitted that they had made a mistake the argument would end'.

However, when pushed to state the best possible outcome A might say 'If B were to apologise and assure me that this would not happen again the argument would end' and B might say 'If A acknowledged their mistake and offered me some generous compensation the argument would end'.

The point here is that although we rarely achieve the best possible outcome in an argument, we will always try to achieve it, and even if an argument is unlikely to be resolved, we won't bother to engage in the dialogue if we don't consider the best possible outcome a possibility, however remote.

If an actor is saying the lines but not actively trying to gain the best possible outcome, this will be clearly visible to the other actors and the audience. This is sometimes referred to as playing to lose. A good actor will have a precisely defined Objective and will always play to win!

A five-year-old child may shout and scream for more sweets even if they can see that the jar is empty – they are playing to win. A husband may collapse onto his knees begging his wife not to leave him, trying as hard as he can because he believes that there is still a possibility she may stay – he is playing to win. If he thought his Objective was absolutely impossible to achieve he wouldn't beg her to stay. He would do or say something else to attempt to satisfy his needs.

A teenager and her mother might argue when the mother enters her daughter's bedroom without knocking. Initially one may decide that the daughter's Objective is for her mother to leave the room and one may decide that the mother's Objective is for her daughter to speak to her without raising her voice. Let's consider the outcomes of these Objectives:

If the mother leaves the room straight away but is clearly upset, the daughter will probably be unsatisfied. If the daughter stops raising her voice and quietly tells her mother that she doesn't want to speak to her, the mother will probably be unsatisfied.

Further interrogation may reveal that the daughter's Objective is for her mother to treat her more like an adult by allowing her a greater level of freedom and privacy (this may include the initial Objective of leaving her room or it may include the Objective of her mother agreeing to knock in future). The mother's Objective may be for her daughter to always allow constructive dialogue between them (this will include the initial Objective of the daughter not raising her voice). We can see here that smaller Objectives will often be part of a larger Objective. We also see that both practical and personal levels of the Objective are present.

Think about an argument you have had or witnessed. You should be able to define words or Actions that either person could have done or said which would have satisfied the other.

The course of the dialogue will change as each person resists the other's attempt to achieve their Objective. This is because the two larger Objectives (the Overall Objectives) will be in some kind of conflict.

Dramatic Units

The changing of smaller Objectives within a larger piece of text can be used to divide the text into sections; these are sometimes called Dramatic Units.

Exercise 1.1

Here is a short script. A & B have Overall Objectives: things they want from the other person. Define an Overall Objective for each in terms of 'what I want the other person to *DO* or *SAY*'.

Next, try to find the smaller Objectives; this will divide the script into Dramatic Units. Once the smaller Objective has changed, the focus of the conflict will have changed. Conflict is at the root of all drama, so this marks a Dramatic Unit.

A   Have you seen the hammer?

B   Ah, I lent it to a friend of mine.

A   Who?

B   Steve.

A   Steve?

B   Yeah.

A   But I need it to fix the gate!

B   He's coming over tomorrow; I'll ask him to bring it with him.

A   That's my hammer!

B   Sorry.

A   I need it today!

B   He'll be over tomorrow.

A   That's no good. It's my hammer. Why did you lend it to Steve?

B   I didn't think you'd mind.

A   You should have asked me first.

B   Yeah, sorry.

A   What am I going to do about the gate?

B   Fix it tomorrow?

A   I'm not here tomorrow. The gate's hanging off the fence. It's dangerous!

B   Sorry.

A   Have you lent any more of my tools to anyone?

B   I don't think so...

A   You don't think so?

B   No.

A   Don't you know??

B   I'm fairly sure I haven't.

A   I don't believe this!

The choice of Objectives and the division of a script into Dramatic Units is highly subjective, so there will be many solutions to this analysis.   Here's one interpretation of A's Objectives, Unit Objectives are in bold whilst individual line Objectives are in italics.

UNIT 1

A   Have you seen the hammer? **To make B give him the hammer**

B   Ah, I lent it to a friend of mine.

UNIT 2

A   Who? **To make B reveal who has the hammer and to make him acknowledge that he should not have taken it or lent it to anyone**

B   Steve.

UNIT 3

A   Steve? **To make B admit that Steve was not a good person to lend the hammer to**

B   Yeah.

UNIT 4

A   But I need it to fix the gate! **To make B apologise and offer to get it back**

B   He's coming over tomorrow; I'll ask him to bring it with him.

A   That's my hammer! *To make B acknowledge that 'asking' Steve isn't enough, he should be told to return the hammer*

B   Sorry.

A   I need it today! *To make B offer to go and get it*

B   He'll be over tomorrow.

A   That's no good. It's my hammer! *To make B acknowledge that an apology isn't enough.*

UNIT 5

A   Why did you lend it to Steve? **To make B admit that he has done wrong**

B   I didn't think you'd mind.

A   You should have asked me first. *To make B acknowledge this*

B   Yeah, sorry.

UNIT 6

A   What am I going to do about the gate? **To make B acknowledge the implications of his actions and show repentance**

B   Fix it tomorrow?

A   I'm not here tomorrow. The gate's hanging off the fence. It's dangerous! *To make B acknowledge the seriousness of his mistake*

B   Sorry.

UNIT 7

A   Have you lent any more of my tools to anyone? **To make B acknowledge his culpability and to give assurance that he won't do it again**

B   I don't think so...

UNIT 8

A   You don't think so? **To make B acknowledge his own incompetence and commit to being more trustworthy and reliable**

B   No.

A   Don't you know?? *To make B acknowledge his incompetence and his lack of respect for A's equipment*

B   I'm fairly sure I haven't.

A   I don't believe this! *To make B acknowledge how exceptional his behaviour has been*

Once we've arrived at a list of Unit Objectives, we can see how they combine towards an Overall Objective. In the case of A it might be something like 'to make B apologise and submit to A's authority' or 'to make B show respect and commit to asking before taking A's tools'.

A line without at least one Objective will lack a layer of truth and a character without underlying Character Objectives will be flat and lifeless, so making choices will always produce something more interesting and lifelike than making none. Stronger choices will lead to more colourful and dramatic results.

Chapter 2: Overcoming Obstacles

Some Objectives will be relatively easy to achieve while others will require considerably more effort. This can be more easily dealt with if we clearly define these difficulties as Obstacles which need to be overcome in order to achieve the Objective.

An Objective with a high level of importance must be strived for with force and/or tactical precision, in spite of, and sometimes in direct conflict with, the Obstacles that stand in its way. An Objective of relatively low importance will be abandoned more readily in the face of challenging Obstacles. A greater level of dramatic intensity is attained when an Objective of high importance is pursued in the face of substantial Obstacles.

Let's consider the Objective behind the line 'Will you lend me some money?' spoken by A to B.

There will be a practical Objective such as 'to get the other person to lend me money' accompanied by a personal Objective such as 'to get the other person to confirm that they still respect me'. These can be combined more usefully as 'to get the other person to lend me some money while maintaining their respect for me'.

If B is a trusted friend then an Obstacle might be that their trust in A is jeopardised a little by making this request; this is a risk attached to the Objective and it will be more effectively dealt with as an Obstacle which needs to be overcome.

How might this affect the delivery of the line? Perhaps A will maintain more direct eye contact with B as a way of gaining trust or use a calm and reassuring tone. The important point is that the actor doesn't calculate or anticipate employing these subtle details; they instead focus on overcoming the Obstacle (of trust being in jeopardy) while the subtleties of the delivery occur naturally.

We can increase the magnitude of this Obstacle by imagining that this is the third time in a week that A has asked B for money. As the Obstacle grows, effective delivery of the line requires more effort and care if a realistic attempt to achieve the Objective is made. Again, the subtle variations in the delivery are not considered by the actor in advance but are produced naturally as the actor focuses on trying to achieve the Objective amid the terrain of new and greater Obstacles.

Let's imagine that B is in an impoverished state. This presents a different Obstacle, but one that makes pursuing the Objective equally, if not more, difficult than in the previous situation.

So now let's imagine that both of the above Obstacles are present and let's add an extra Obstacle: the person asking for money (A) knows that if they don't borrow the money they will be forced to go to prison later that day. As the level of importance and the urgency of the Objective increases, so does the amount of effort and care taken to achieve that Objective.

Let's change the circumstances a little and imagine that B has only known A for a week or two. While the Objective may remain the same as, or similar to, the previous situation, there will be a new and significant Obstacle present: the level of trust required for a loan may not yet be established. This will make the line particularly difficult to deliver.

Don't Play the Obstacle

When an actor is new to working with Obstacles, there can be a tendency to struggle with the Obstacle in the moments before the line and then to say the line with relative ease, as if the Obstacle is a hurdle which exists independently from the line. But in real life we may struggle to speak when dealing with an appreciable Obstacle, with some words being significantly more difficult to say than others. Although the Obstacle will be present before the line, its resistance will remain present throughout the speaking of the line.

The difficulty for the actor is that these Obstacles are often character traits and conditions, and there can be a tendency for the actor to display the particular trait to show the Obstacle, but this is not truthful. The effort should be in overcoming the Obstacle and not in showing it. The key is to focus on achieving the Objective, even if the script tells you that it is not achieved; the character doesn't know this and will be 'playing to win' whatever Obstacles are present.

In making an apology there will usually be an Obstacle such as pride or reluctance to admit failure. This will affect the delivery of the apology, but the speaker will be making every effort to overcome their pride.

Imagine someone is making an apology while maintaining a strong sense of personal pride. The apology will appear insincere. If the Objective is being played truthfully then the Obstacle of pride must be truthfully overcome, and this will require effort. Instead of 'showing' that the pride is being overcome, the actor must trust that the audience will perceive the subtlety of these dynamics.

Imagine A is confronting B, who has a bad temper and a violent reputation. A will find that fear of B is an Obstacle but A will use maximum effort to hide the fear and will try to overcome it. If B sees that A is fearful, the confrontation will have little or no effect.

In real life we try to overcome the Obstacles which prevent us from getting what we want, and it is the same with acting: the effort is used to overpower the Obstacle. If the above example were part of a performance, the audience may not see the fear but they will see the effort made in order to hide it.

This can be seen physically in someone with an injury which causes a limp. They will walk as well as they possibly can and their main effort will be to minimise the effect of the limp; they are trying to overcome the Obstacle. We see a change in their gait but what we mainly see is that their focus is on overcoming the limp.

Someone who is drunk won't willingly sway and slur their words; they will be trying to walk in a straight line and speak as coherently as possible. We may notice them swaying and slurring but we will see the great effort they make to appear sober. This will be most apparent when they have an Objective which relies on them being sober: perhaps they are trying to convince a policeman that they are well enough to make their own way home, or to convince a bartender that they should be served another drink!

Try improvising asking for a loan from the postman or a neighbour who you don't really know: you should feel the awkwardness that negotiation of the Obstacle brings. It is important to truthfully 'play the Objective' by actually trying to get them to agree to lend you the money (playing to win) and to not just 'go through the motions' of asking the question and expecting a refusal (playing to lose). It is also important not to 'play the Obstacle' by focusing on displaying the awkwardness; attempting to overcome the Obstacle and to achieve the Objective will produce a far more truthful performance.

The Obstacles in the above example all relate to characteristics or conditions that concern B: their trust in A, their reluctance to make continual loans and their current poverty. These are Obstacles existing outside A and can be referred to as external Obstacles.

An Obstacle which is present inside A is referred to as an internal Obstacle, for example A's pride. If A's character is a little different it might be their shame that represents an internal Obstacle. In other words, A must overcome their pride or their shame in order to say the line.

Think about how difficult it can be to make an apology or to admit that you have made a serious mistake. These difficulties are often due to internal Obstacles.

Now think about how difficult it can be to make somebody else realise and acknowledge that they have made a mistake, or to get them to question a long-held belief. These Objectives will be obstructed by external Obstacles.

Exercise 2.1

Try improvising an awkward apology and see where the effort is experienced. Now improvise making someone else, a particularly confident person, acknowledge their mistake and see where this effort is experienced. There should be a clear difference between how it feels to overcome an Obstacle within oneself and overcoming an Obstacle within somebody else; the focus of the effort will be internal or external.

Exercise 2.2

The following scene has no context. Choose a situation and divide the scene into Units. For A and B derive Objectives for each unit and finally Obstacles.

A   What time is it?

B   10 o'clock

A   Are you ready?

B   Yes, you?

A   I think so

B   Let's go

A   OK

B   OK

Try choosing different situations for this script, with different Objectives and Obstacles.

Exercise 2.3

Consider the line 'What are you doing?'

Find a context, an Objective and an Obstacle for the line.

Now replace the Obstacle for one of a different strength. Do this several times and try to rank each Obstacle from 1 to 10 in its level of difficulty.

Example

A woman is speaking to her husband. He has just got out of bed in the middle of the night and is looking in the top drawer of his wardrobe. The noise has woken her up.

Her Objective is to get him to agree that he'll come back to bed soon.

Here are three possible Obstacles:

Her Obstacle (level 1) is that she doesn't want to wake herself up any more by speaking to him.

Her Obstacle (level 5) is that she doesn't want to start an argument; this will definitely disturb her sleep.

Her Obstacle (level 8) is fear; she knows he keeps a loaded gun in the drawer.

Remember not to 'display' the Obstacle but to focus on overcoming it in order to achieve your Objective.

Exercise 2.4

Divide the following script into Units. Find two different situations for the script, a low-stakes situation and a high-stakes situation. Work out Objectives for both characters and try to keep the Objectives the same for both situations.

Now find Obstacles for both characters for each Unit but make them fairly small in the low-stakes situation and substantial in the high-stakes situation.

A   I have to leave.

B   Really?

A   There are things I need to do.

B   I thought we were going to have a talk.

A   I've been thinking, and I've made a decision.

B   Well?

A   Well.

B   Are you going to tell me what you've decided?

A   Come on; you know.

B   Really?

A   Really.

B   Well, close the door when you go.

Imagine a policeman knocking at a door to deliver these lines:

'Are you Mrs Elizabeth Hutchinson?'

'I'm sorry to tell you that your son Thomas has been killed in a road traffic accident.'

The Obstacles here are clearly difficult to overcome, and one can imagine a young police officer struggling very much in the moments before reaching the door. Once they have knocked on the door, the Obstacle may grow rapidly, and when they are facing the mother the Obstacle to the police officer's Objective may appear to be almost insurmountable. But to say the actual words, especially the word 'killed', will be extremely difficult indeed.

We should note that in an Emotionally intense situation like this it can be tempting to ignore the Objective but the Objective must be clearly defined and a considerable effort should be made to truthfully achieve it, otherwise the actor's focus will be entirely on the Obstacle and a clumsy and sentimental delivery will result. Consider what the Objective might be in this situation: 'to get the mother to calmly accept the unexpected death of her son' seems almost impossible to achieve, but this kind of situation will always present huge Obstacles, and an effective delivery involving the negotiation of such Obstacles in a truthful attempt to achieve the Objective will undoubtedly produce intense drama.

The essence of all drama is conflict and a line without an Obstacle will be lacking an element of conflict; the presence of an Obstacle will make the character drive the line with more purpose.

A good actor needs to be able to effectively identify Obstacles and, through practice, get in the habit of placing focus and effort on using the words to overcome them. Dealing with a complex array of Obstacles at the same time can lead to a loss of clarity in the delivery, so restricting the dynamic to one or two Obstacles will be perfectly sufficient.

Chapter 3: Actioning

The term Actioning has become fundamental to all modern actor training. Playing an Objective rigorously means that the actor will be trying to make the person, or people, that they're speaking to *FEEL* something and, as a consequence of that feeling, to *DO* or *SAY* something very specific. The speaker is using words to make something happen to somebody else and the precise way in which they are doing this is defined as the Action that they are using.

Let's look again at the short and well-used phrase 'Hello' being spoken to different people. The first may be a particularly good friend whom the speaker has not seen for a considerable time. Imagine how the speaker might say 'Hello' to this person.

The second 'Hello' might be to someone with whom the speaker has recently had a strong disagreement. How might this 'Hello' be spoken?

The third might be said to someone with whom the speaker was socialising the night before; this person had become very drunk and did some embarrassing things. How might this 'Hello' be said?

You can probably imagine how each 'Hello' might be said, but let's take a look at what is actually happening.

In the first instance the speaker's Objective might be 'to get the other person to recognise me and show joy and enthusiasm at our impromptu meeting'. A simple and direct way to do this will be to *Excite* them.

In the second instance the speaker's Objective might be 'to make the other person take an initial step towards resolving our state of conflict'. A way to achieve this might be to *Confront* them.

In the third instance the speaker's Objective might be 'to get the other person to show remorse and humility'. This may be achieved if the speaker *Shames* them.

Now let's see what happens to the Actions if we change the Objectives for each situation.

In the first instance the speaker's alternative Objective might be 'to make the other person laugh with me'. The Action here might be to *Surprise*, *Shock* or *Tease* them. (Note that using each one of these Actions will produce a distinct, specific and different expression of the phrase 'Hello' even though they may all be attempts to pursue the same Objective.)

In the second instance the speaker's alternative Objective might be 'to make the other person go away without entering into discussion'. This may be achieved by using one of the Actions *Dismiss*, *Disown* or *Reject*. (Each of these will also produce different effects but may be used to pursue the same Objective.)

In the third instance the speaker's alternative Objective might be 'to make the other person apologise in the strongest terms'. In this case the speaker might *Scold*, *Reprimand* or *Condemn* the other person. As before, these three Actions will produce different, distinct and specific effects, but all will be aiming towards the same Objective.

These words are often referred to as Action verbs but they are actually *Transitive Verbs*. This is because the Action is transitory: one person performs the Action but its effect happens to someone, or something else.

I *Shame* you: I do the *Shaming* but you feel *Shamed*.

You *Reject* me: you do the *Rejecting* but I feel *Rejected*.

She *Inspires* him: she does the *Inspiring* but he feels *Inspired*.

He *Excites* her: he does the *Exciting* but she feels *Excited*.

We use *Transitive Verbs* all the time, although sometimes the importance of the Objective may not be enough for the Action to be obvious. However, in an argument the *Transitive Verbs* will be strong and clearly defined and will often change frequently.

Here is an argument with some suggestions for *Transitive Verbs:*

A   Did you make that mess in the kitchen? *Challenge*

B   I'll clear it up in the morning. *Dismiss*

A   I need to use the kitchen now. *Confront*

B   My mess isn't in your way. I've been working all day, I'll do it in the morning. *Appease*

A   You never have to work around my mess because I clean it up straight away! *Berate*

B   Please, I'm tired. *Implore*

A   Tired? You're just lazy! *Mock*

B   Relax! It's not my fault that you're stressed out. *Soothe*

A   I can't relax when I'm trying to cook in a dirty kitchen! *Scold*

B   You can never relax! *Condemn*

A   I'm going out! *Reject*

B   Where are you going? *Entreat*

A   Somewhere clean and tidy! *Repel*

Note: for the line 'My mess isn't in your way. I've been working all day, I'll do it in the morning', three *Transitive Verbs* might be used, one for each part of the line, e.g. 'My mess isn't in your way' (*Disarm*), 'I've been working all day' (*Implore*) and 'I'll do it in the morning' (*Pacify*).

This level of detail may be found in most, if not all text but analysis at this level can be time consuming and laborious. It is therefore only necessary when a complex line of this nature sounds or feels flat and untruthful. After significant training with *Transitive Verbs* most actors will automatically find this level of variety anyway.

Exercise 3.1

Try making up a different sequence of *Transitive Verbs* for the same argument. It might start like this:

A   Did you make that mess in the kitchen? *Tease*

B   I'll clear it up in the morning. *Appease*

A   I need to use the kitchen now. *Encourage*

You can see how the same script will have a completely different dramatic structure if it takes a different path of *Transitive Verbs.*

The following game is an excellent way for actors to develop precision and range in their use of *Transitive Verbs*.

The Shop Game

Exercise 3.2

Actors A and B improvise a shop scenario. B is behind the counter working in the shop and A is a customer.

A has prepared a list of *Transitive Verbs* in advance and chooses one without telling B what it is.

A walks into the shop and delivers a neutral line such as 'I'd like a pint of milk and a loaf of bread' while deploying the *Transitive Verb*. (The line does not include 'Hi' or 'please' as it needs to be neutral.)

B then makes one attempt to guess the *Transitive Verb*. If B is correct, the actors swap roles and play again.

If B's guess is incorrect, and this will happen much of the time, A must walk into the shop and say the line again, but this time they'll be deploying the *Transitive Verb* which B incorrectly suggested. Then A will repeat the exercise using the original *Transitive Verb* and B will make another attempt at guessing correctly.

This rapidly improves an actor's precision with *Transitive Verbs* because they are exploring and expressing the subtle differences between a tight range of similar but distinctly different Actions.

For example, the game might go like this:

A uses *Accuse* with the line 'I'd like a pint of milk and a loaf of bread'.

B guesses *Intimidate* and is told by A that this is not the *Transitive Verb* that was being used.

A then uses *Intimidate* with the line. (Both A and B will notice a subtle difference.)

A then repeats the original *Transitive Verb, Accuse.*

B guesses *Threaten* and is told by A that this is not the *Transitive Verb* that was being used.

A then uses *Threaten* with the line. (Again both A and B will notice a subtle difference.)

A then repeats the original *Transitive Verb, Accuse.*

B guesses *Accuse* and the roles are reversed, with B choosing from their list of *Transitive Verbs* and A going behind the counter in the shop.

What happens is that each time A uses a similar but slightly different *Transitive Verb*, the subtle differences are discovered, and each time A returns to *Accuse* they will become a little more precise.

Here's another example of how the game might go:

A uses *Charm* with the line 'I'd like a pint of milk and a loaf of bread'.

B guesses *Comfort* and is told by A that this is not the *Transitive Verb* that was being used.

A uses *Comfort* with the line. (Both A and B will notice a subtle difference.)

A then repeats the original *Transitive Verb*, *Charm*.

B guesses *Tease* and is told by A that this is not the *Transitive Verb* that was being used.

A uses *Tease* with the line. (Again both A and B will notice a distinct yet subtle difference.)

A then repeats the original *Transitive Verb, Charm*.

B guesses *Charm* and the roles are reversed, with B choosing from their list of *Transitive Verbs* and A standing behind the counter in the shop.

The game may last much longer than these examples while exploring just one *Transitive Verb* before it is guessed correctly; many similar, but distinctly different, Actions will be used and both actors' range and skill with *Transitive Verbs* will be increased.

Exercise 3.3

Play the game with both actors sharing the following short list of *Transitive Verbs:*

Accuse   Threaten   Comfort   Excite   Condemn   Dismiss
Belittle   Taunt   Undermine   Invite   Inspire   Intrigue

The key to playing Actions truthfully is not to plan in advance **how** you're going to say the line but to focus entirely on making the other person **feel** the verb. It helps to imagine how you want them to react (i.e. the expression you will see on their face if they are *Condemned* or *Excited*), then use the words to make sure they react in this way.

36

Exercise 3.4

Using the following script, find a *Transitive Verb* for each line. You will need to imagine a situation with Overall Objectives for each character. Don't assign Obstacles in this exercise; for the moment it's best to just focus on using the *Transitive Verbs*.

A   Do you see that?

B   What should we do?

A   Let's just wait and see what happens.

B   I think we should go.

A   We can't just walk away.

B   I don't really want to be involved.

A   Well I'm not going to just leave.

B   Look, it's fine now.

A   That was close.

B   I need a drink.

Since we all use *Transitive Verbs* anyway it may seem pointless to use them as part of an actor's training, but their continued and practised use will take the actor's focus away from themselves and onto the person or people they are talking to.

In the real world everyone has their own 'set' of *Transitive Verbs*, a group of Actions which they use on a daily basis. There will be some Actions which an individual is not familiar with and there will be many Actions that an individual has never used.

For example, some of us may be used to *Intimidating* people but not used to *Comforting* them. Others may have the opposite approach: they are used to *Comforting* people but are unfamiliar with *Intimidating* them.

An individual's personal 'set' of *Transitive Verbs* will be governed by many factors such as class, culture, gender, education and family. For example, someone from a middle-class family who's been privately educated in the British public-school system may be likely to have more *Transitive Verbs* associated with 'high status' in their repertoire than someone from a deprived inner-city area. The person from the deprived area may be likely to have more *Transitive Verbs* which suggest 'struggle'. This will be in some part due to the factors necessary for success and survival within each environment. Whereas the middle-class person may be used to

Commanding or *Challenging*, the working-class person may be more used to *Confronting* or *Demanding*. (Although this is an overly simplistic example it illustrates how differing *Transitive Verb* use can help to create a fundamental part of a character's colour and texture.)

An actor needs to have a very wide array of *Transitive Verbs* available as this will allow a much wider range of expression within a greater variety of dramatic situations. An ideal way to do this is to regularly play the Shop Game using an ever-widening range of *Transitive Verbs*.

Once an actor has a large vocabulary of *Transitive Verbs*, they can choose a set of Actions which will suit a specific character. This will give the character colour and continuity, and it will allow for a very distinct difference between each character the actor develops.

Exercise 3.5

With two characters, A and B, write a six-line script using the following sequence of *Transitive Verbs*, one for each line. Now think of a new situation with different characters and write another six-line script using the same *Transitive Verbs*. Now do it a third time with yet another new situation, characters and script but with the same *Transitive Verbs*.

Implore   Placate   Demand   Scold   Condemn   Subdue

When you perform each of the three scripts, you will notice that although the text, characters, situation and Objectives are different, the dramatic structure will be the same across all three. In many ways the text, characters, situation and Objectives become secondary to the drama, which is actually driven by the Actions, the *Transitive Verbs*.

Chapter 4: Advanced Actioning

Actioning using *Transitive Verbs* helps to solve many of the common issues that an actor will often struggle with; it does this by clearly placing the focus, attention and performance energy onto the other person, thereby taking the actor's focus away from themselves. This allows for unmonitored, and therefore more natural behaviour, both physically and psychologically, from the actor.

So far, we have dealt with realistic and achievable Actions using *Transitive Verbs* which have a genuine psychological effect: *Shame, Reject, Inspire, Excite* etc. In these cases the person being spoken to may really feel *Shamed, Rejected, Inspired or Excited*. For the most part this is exactly what we do in real life: we use our words to make other people feel very specific things, and we do this with the intention that their feelings will make them behave in a way which will help us to achieve our Objectives.

But what happens if we try using *Transitive Verbs* which are not realistically achievable, for example if we play Actions which are not psychological but physical?

Let's look at the *Transitive Verb LEVITATE*. What happens if you try to lift somebody off the ground using nothing but words?

Well, in the real world you might assume that this is not possible, so you would not really make the necessary effort.

But if you 'play to win', as a good actor will, by truthfully trying to achieve your Objective (to make the other person rise from the ground) and focusing your energy on overcoming the Obstacle (the laws of physics), the effect will be intense and dramatic, commanding the attention of the audience. The effort being made by the actor will be extreme because the Obstacle is so difficult, if not impossible, to overcome.

The important point is that an observer will believe that the performer believes that this can be achieved.

I will refer to these Actions as *Abstract Transitive Verbs*.

The *Transitive Verb LEVITATE* is an extreme example and might be useful if the actor is playing someone with magical powers, or someone who thinks they have magical powers. But we have a huge array of *Non-Psychological Transitive Verbs* to choose from, and they will each have a different and often very unusual or powerful effect.

Consider trying to *FREEZE* somebody with words or perhaps to *MELT* them. A simplistic solution might be to assume that, as these Actions are all impossible to achieve using only words, the effort will be half-hearted and generalised. But if the actor is 'playing to win', the specific characteristics of each impossible Action will be seen.

FREEZING involves a structural change from malleability to brittleness through a mechanism of energy reduction (cooling) within the other person; *MELTING* involves a structural change from some kind of solidity to liquidity through a mechanism of energy increase (heating) within the other person.

What the actor is actually trying to do is to use words to draw energy from, or add energy to, the other person in order to have a very specific effect.

If the actor is truthfully attempting to make this change in another person, these dynamics will be in some way present in their Action.

Let's look at the contrast between *Burn* and *Stroke*. To *Burn* involves imparting energy with some aggression while feeding it with oxygen; to *Stroke* involves making the other person feel the gentle and flowing sensations of touch.

There are many differences in terms of energy, intensity, weight and rhythm between these two Actions. These differences can clearly be seen when the Actions are played one after the other.

The exact technical accuracy of the physical effects of *Abstract Transitive Verbs* is not that important; what is important is to have your own idea of the specific effects which you are trying to illicit in the person you are talking to and endeavouring to make them happen.

Exercise 4.1

Try playing the Shop Game with *Abstract Transitive Verbs* using the following list:

Stroke	*Burn*	*Melt*	*Crush*	*Dissolve*	*Grind*
Freeze	*Thaw*	*Desiccate*	*Levitate*	*Flatten*	*Elevate*

You will find that *Levitate* and *Elevate* are remarkably similar but as an actor learns to be more specific in their Actioning the differences will be more noticeable.

Abstract Transitive Verbs are particularly useful when a special or intense effect is called for. At the end of a vicious argument when perhaps one character says to the other 'I hate you!' the effect can be amplified and intensified if an *Abstract Transitive Verb* such as *Destroy*, *Crush* or even *Vapourise* is used.

Superheroes, magical beings or mythical creatures can be made more ethereal and other-worldly while maintaining a truthful integrity through the use of *Abstract Transitive Verbs*.

Actioning Without Words

When guiding students through the Shop Game, I often ask them to play the action, the *Transitive Verb*, as soon as they walk in and when they are standing at the counter before delivering the line. This means that the actor will be using their entire body and mind in an attempt to affect the other person in the specific way denoted by the *Transitive Verb*, and because the vast majority of their focus will be on the other person, their body will be 'telling the truth' in a less self-conscious and more honest way.

The Shop Game can be played without any words at all, and with *Abstract Transitive Verbs* in addition to *Psychological Transitive Verbs.* An actor armed with the Action *Stretch* will walk into the shop while focusing as much of their body and mind on *Stretching* the other person. This will be visible in the way that they hold themselves, the various parameters of the way that they move and the expression with which they look at the other person. But it will be most apparent in its effect on the person working in the shop.

Once an actor has attempted the Action, I will often ask the person behind the counter 'How do you feel?'

The answer will usually be complex and highly nuanced, but it will invariably include characteristics of the *Transitive Verb* which is being used.

It may take many different guesses, which will allow several other Actions to be explored, before the Action that was originally being played is finally discovered.

In real life we've all seen a 'look that could kill' or malicious intent in somebody's walk. We've seen the concern and care of a parent rushing to comfort an injured child or the 'look of love' that can say more than any words, perhaps from lovers reunited at a railway platform after a long separation. These are examples of how *Abstract Transitive Verbs* are used in daily life.

Exercise 4.2

Try playing the Shop Game with *Abstract Transitive Verbs* but without any words, using the following list:

Stroke	*Burn*	*Melt*	*Crush*	*Dissolve*	*Grind*
Freeze	*Thaw*	*Desiccate*	*Levitate*	*Flatten*	*Elevate*

It is important to avoid miming or making artificial gestures; for example, when using the *Transitive Verb STROKE*, avoid stroking the air with your hands. Try to 'allow' your body to be relaxed, centred and truthful.

Playing *Abstract Transitive Verbs* without using text will often force an actor to behave outside of the usual limits of their physicality. In the same way that we can expand our individual set of psychological Actions, we can also increase and enhance the range of our physical expression by using *Abstract Transitive Verbs* without words.

Chapter 5: Response

Up to this point we have looked at Actioning, the use of *Transitive Verbs*, both Psychological and Abstract, and the overcoming of Obstacles as a way to achieve Objectives. These mechanisms are all part of a character's attempt to affect the other person or persons with whom they are interacting, and they all involve the use of energy, effort and information being directed from the character towards the other person or people.

But how does a character know how successful an attempt to achieve the Objective has been? Once an effort has been made to affect the other person or people, the character needs to receive some feedback before assessing the next step in their attempt to achieve their Objective. This is where Response comes into play. In Response mode the speaker is trying to get information and energy to flow from the listener back to the speaker.

When an actor is working with a script it can be difficult not to see the character's journey in a linear way because the journey is the same every time the script is read or performed. An actor will know how the other person is going to respond because the script, along with the direction and the rehearsal process, has already made this clear.

The following line is linear, or so it appears, but with each piece of punctuation comes the potential for a Response from the other character.

A   Don't go. Come back! Steve!

In fact, the line has the potential to develop in an infinite number of ways. Here is a map showing a few possibilities with different Responses from B presented in each column:

So, we see that an actor saying the simple line 'Don't go. Come back! Steve!' needs to acknowledge the 'infinite space' that exists after each phrase.

Anything can happen in this moment; the Objective may become more tangible or a new Obstacle may be presented. I sometimes refer to this moment as 'no man's land'.

Actors will often simply pretend that they don't know how the other person will respond, and this is sometimes done in a passive way. For example, an actor might pause after a sentence, in order to give the impression that they are allowing a possible Response from the other person, before continuing with their next piece of dialogue.

In reality the search for Response is not passive but highly active. When we are using dialogue to pursue an Objective, we hunt energetically for information which will reveal what the other person feels and thinks in Response to our words; through their expression we will try to 'read their mind'.

Exercise 5.1

Try observing social groups in a cafe or a bar. When one person is addressing the group, perhaps telling a story or a joke, note how they look at individuals within the group. You will see that the people being spoken to will usually be showing signs that they're listening in Response to the speaker. (These may be tiny nods, smiles or eyebrows raised in interest.)

You will see that the speaker needs these signals in order to keep their dialogue going; the signals 'feed' the speaker and tell them that their Objectives are within reach.

If the people in the group give bored looks in Response, or even avoid eye contact with the speaker, then the speaker will usually stop speaking.

You may notice that as the dialogue progresses the speaker will exclude the people who are not giving interested nods and focus on those who are responding most positively.

The speaker is **actively hunting** for signs of positive Response.

Exercise 5.2

(This exercise may seem a little cruel so please only use it with an actor and explain to them what you've been doing when you finish so that they too may benefit from the experience.)

Ask someone to tell you about something: an interesting event or a film they've recently enjoyed. When they are talking to you they will be hunting for Response, but force yourself not to nod, smile or show signs of interest. As long as you are strict in your lack of positive Response, they should find it very difficult to continue.

Breathing and the Diaphragm in Response Mode

The diaphragm is a thin sheet of muscle crossing the thorax just below the lungs. As it contracts, air is drawn into the lungs and when it is relaxed, air is expelled from the lungs. Although its primary function is to provide oxygen for respiration, it is also used to govern air pressure through the vocal folds for generating voice sounds and for rapid in-breath in the middle of speech.

The diaphragm, through the phrenic nerve, is connected to the entire central nervous system and each will be affected by the other.

An impact to the solar plexus, which is situated in the immediate vicinity of the diaphragm, will often cause difficulty in breathing as it interferes with the correct operation of the diaphragm.

Feelings of fear or apprehension can also cause fluctuation in the diaphragm, sometimes referred to as 'butterflies in the stomach'. The diaphragm is an extremely sensitive area.

Because the diaphragm is an area of potential vulnerability, affecting the entire body, there can be a tendency to hold a little tension in this muscle as a form of self-protection. This is very common in people who are in a stressed or nervous situation; it can be a way of inhibiting the fluctuations (butterflies) caused by apprehension or the anticipation of something challenging.

Tension in the diaphragm is the enemy of the actor not only because it inhibits the flow of nervous information between the body, the voice and the brain but also because it stops the truthful hunt for Response.

In Response mode we are trying to read what someone is thinking in order to assess the impact of our Action. We need to be open, sensitive and receptive, so we will release our diaphragm as freely as the situation will allow. To fully release the diaphragm requires the acceptance of a certain degree of vulnerability.

Exercise 5.3

Place your palm loosely on your belly and shout 'Hey!' as if you are calling to someone on the other side of the road; imagine someone who's looking the other way and you're trying to make them respond. You should feel your abdomen pulse inwards as you make the sound and then release outwards afterwards. This release will leave a relaxed diaphragm and allow the free flow of nervous information between the body and brain and, more importantly, between the speaker and the listener .

We often go into Response mode when we start to watch a film. We will sit down, make ourselves comfortable and often let out a big, relaxed sigh as the film starts. Releasing the diaphragm is a way of allowing the film to affect us by being open and allowing vulnerability.

When someone asks a question they will release their diaphragm at the question mark. It may be very brief as they may follow up with another question, but if they really want an answer the diaphragmatic release will be there.

Response and Punctuation

Punctuation separates Thoughts. A full stop, a question mark or an exclamation mark (final punctuation) will signify the end of a Thought, and other punctuation will show how Thoughts are connected. Since each Thought in a section of dialogue will be generated by the speaker in an attempt to achieve the Objective, the speaker will usually try to assess the impact of the Action generated by this Thought by checking for Response in the listener at the punctuation.

A question mark is especially important as it explicitly requires a Response.

Exercise 5.4

Ask someone to present you with a list: perhaps 10 countries they would like to visit, their five favourite meals or the ingredients needed to make a complex meal.

While they are talking try to observe the moments when they look for Response; in many cases they will look to you for Response at every piece of punctuation.

Public Speaking

Think about the most interesting teachers, lecturers or public speakers; they will actively engage the audience by truthfully looking for Response, usually asking real questions. The most boring ones will use rhetorical questions and will rarely look for Response. Successful political speakers will make the listeners feel that their Response is needed, and the listeners will feel as though they are an intrinsic part of the speaker's Objective. This will make the listeners feel valued by the speaker and they will be more likely to pay attention to the speaker's words.

Exceptions

There will of course be situations where the speaker isn't looking for a Response, where the Objective lies outside of the person being spoken to.

Imagine someone buying a ticket for a train which is already on the platform. Their Overall Objective is to get on the train, so the Objective behind their dialogue is to get the person selling the ticket to put it into their hand as quickly as possible.

Someone might be talking loudly to you but their Objective might involve being overheard by someone nearby who they're trying to impress.

A rude and officious bank manager might want to avoid giving you an overdraft; their Objective may be to make you decide to go to a different bank.

An unfriendly waiter may ask how your meal was but may have no interest in your Response; their Objective may be to finish work early and go to the cinema.

A self-indulgent artist may talk about their success to someone at a party; their Objective may be to 'be seen' by as many people as possible.

The important point is that these choices should be within the actor's control, making a wider variety of character, colour and truthful dramatic content available.

Chapter 6: Action–Response–Thought (A.R.T.)

Whenever someone tries to achieve something in the world outside of themselves, they will use the following sequence of different modes: Action, Response and Thought.

We've looked at Actioning, an individual's attempt to affect someone else in pursuit of an Objective; we've looked at Response, their assessment of the impact of the Action on the other person; and now we come to the final component of the sequence: Thought.

Action	Do something to achieve your Objective
Response	Observe the difference made by this Action
Thought	Calculate what the next Action should be

Imagine someone making a flour, milk and egg mixture, followed by a little oil or melted butter, in order to cook some crepes.

The first Action will be to put some flour into a bowl.

They will then look at the quantity, either using scales to measure or making a rough visual estimate. This is the Response phase.

This will then be followed by one of two or three possible Thoughts: 'This is enough flour', 'This is not enough flour' or 'This is too much flour'.

The Thought then 'drives' the next Action, which will be to start adding the milk, add more flour or remove some flour. Let's imagine that the Thought was 'This is enough flour'; the next Action will be to add milk by measuring or just pouring some in.

Once the milk is added, and perhaps mixed into the flour with a whisk, the person will examine the mixture visually, or by feeling with the whisk, and the Response to this will 'drive' the Thought phase: perhaps something like 'This feels properly mixed' or 'This is still too lumpy'.

As before, this Thought will lead to the next Action: either add more milk or continue mixing in the melted butter or oil.

It can be summed up like this:

Action   Add the flour to the bowl

Response   Check the quantity

Thought   This is enough, I need to add the milk

Action   Add and mix in the milk

Response	Check to see if it's mixed in properly

Thought	It's too lumpy; I need to mix it more

This may seem incredibly obvious and unnecessarily pedantic, but actors will all too often concentrate so fully on Actioning the lines that the Response and Thought phases are neglected.

Thought

One may imagine that Thought is invisible, but this is not the case at all.

If you visit a friend it is easy to tell that they have something on their mind which is troubling them, even if they are trying incredibly hard to hide it. We may not be able to 'read' the exact detail of what they are thinking but we can often judge the importance and, to some degree, the personal impact of those Thoughts.

For the actor it is not enough to 'pretend' to think, because humans, including the audience, are incredibly good at reading the Thoughts of others; the actor must really think, and decisions must really be made. Every line spoken, each Action made by the actor, should be driven by a Thought. It doesn't matter how quick and fleeting the Thought is, but if it is not present the line will lack a layer of truth.

Much of the truth of our experience of the relationships between people happens outside of the words which are spoken; there is as much in the silence of Response and Thought as there is in the Action of the lines. We see the words of a script as the main bulk and substance of the complete event, but if we look at the words as a product of Response and Thought then they are merely symptoms of a larger structure.

Every line, or Action, is driven by a Thought; it is as if the Thought is a stone thrown into a pond and the words are the ripples generated. The real substance here is composed of Thought. The text is merely the articulation of that Thought as a route to achieving an Objective.

A Shakespearean soliloquy is a good example of how the Thought is in fact the root of the text. The writer is using text to allow the audience to experience the Thoughts of the character. In reality the soliloquy would have no words and be entirely composed of Thought.

We have looked at how different the two modes of Action and Response are in terms of the direction of energy and information. We have seen how different they are in terms of their effect on the body of the speaker and we have also seen that they operate in the space between people and that the flow of information is in opposite directions.

Thought occurs in a different kind of mental area, which I refer to as Thought-space. Let's take another look at Exercise 5.4, which involved asking someone to make a list, perhaps the ingredients for cooking a meal.

Once an item from the list has been mentioned (or 'delivered' by Actioning to the listener whose Response has then been noted), we can see that the eyes of the speaker move away from the listener as they go into Thought mode: they appear to 'zone out' momentarily. This is because the attention of the speaker has now left the physical space shared by the listener and themselves as they explore the 'inner space' of their mind in order to find the next item on the list. Once the item has been retrieved from Thought-space their attention is returned to the listener and the sequence moves onto the next phase.

Exercise 6.1

Ask someone to explain something complex, perhaps to do with science or philosophy, and watch them go through the three phases of the cycle.

(Asking someone to explain, in terms of planetary orbits, rotations etc, what makes days, years and seasons is a great example because a clear explanation requires a considerable degree of Thought.)

Note how engaging the Thought phase is to watch, how intriguing it is for the listener to see what is 'fished' from the speaker's mind at the end of this phase.

Discovery

If Exercise 6.1 above is challenging enough for the speaker, you may see Discovery arising from some of the Thoughts. This is one of the most compelling things for humans to observe in others: the realisation of a new and impactful idea.

It is always a pleasure to give people presents but it's especially enjoyable to give presents to children; this is because they are usually unguarded in the honesty of their reactions to the gift.

An adult will carefully unwrap a present and then they will usually give a moderated comment of pleasant surprise and gratitude, whereas a child will tear off the wrapping and show either unrestrained excitement or unconcealed disappointment. It is our observation of the unparalleled energy of Discovery which makes this enjoyable.

We may play a joke on someone precisely to watch this Discovery in action. Someone goes to get a drink from the bar and we hide their phone; when they return we wait to observe the moment when they discover that the phone is no longer where they left it. We observe this Discovery with feigned innocence and await the next moment of Discovery when they realise that they are the victim of a practical joke.

If you are teaching a child about something new, perhaps in maths or science, the teacher's reward is witnessing the moment of Discovery in the child. It is incredibly engaging, as though a light has been switched on in the child's mind.

A moment of Discovery is often accompanied by a deep and sudden inhalation of breath, possibly a way of flooding the brain with oxygen in order to provide energy for new Thoughts which arise from the Discovery. Try to observe how your, and other people's, breath behaves at these moments.

When an actor deals with text, the moments of Discovery should not be missed as they usually form an energetic bridge between the phases of Thought and Action. In terms of space, this is seen by the audience as a jump from Thought-space within one performer's mind to the physical space shared by the performers within the scene: a Eureka moment.

Let's look briefly at the opening lines of Hamlet's famous soliloquy.

He believes that he is alone, Polonius being concealed, so his words, and consequently his Objectives relate to himself: he is trying to make **himself** *DO* or *SAY* something.

If we follow the A.R.T. sequence (Action–Response–Thought) we need to find the Thought that drives the Action of the first line.

There is of course massive scope for every individual actor to find their own interpretation of what that Thought might be, so let's arbitrarily choose the Thought 'suicide would be a way out'.

Hamlet's mind is in turmoil. He is overcome with grief at his father's death, disturbed and confused by the urging of what appears to be his father's ghost and traumatised by his mother's apparent callousness in marrying Claudius so soon after her husband's death. Amidst all of this the sudden realisation that a simple decision must be made can be an enlightening Discovery.

The audience will see the energetic emergence of this Discovery as Hamlet's troubled Thoughts are suddenly distilled and Actioned in the first line:

	Thought	Suicide would be a way out. (Discovery)
To be, or not to be, that is the question;	Action	To make himself decide on life or death
	Response	How shall I decide?
	Thought	I'll look at the first option in detail
Whether 'tis nobler in the mind to suffer The slings and arrows of outrageous fortune,	Action	To make himself consider and accept the reality of living with his pain
	Response	Horror at this notion
	Thought	I need to look at the other option in detail
Or to take arms against a sea of troubles And by opposing end them.	Action	To make himself agree that this is the best solution
	Response	This calms him
	Thought	I will find peace (Potential Discovery)
To die–to sleep;	Action	To make himself accept death easily

	Response	He is reassured
	Thought	Sleep is wonderful (Potential Discovery)
No more;	Action	To make himself glad to die
	Response	Disbelief at how easy it seems
	Thought	I must interrogate this idea more
and by a sleep to say we end The heartache and the thousand natural shocks That flesh is heir to:	Action	Make himself agree that it really is this simple
	Response	Believe that it is that simple
	Thought	I will commit to this
'tis a consummation Devoutly to be wished.	Action	To die by suicide

(The choices made in terms of the Actions, Responses and Thoughts are highly subjective and will have as many permutations as there are actors and directors; those presented in this example are entirely arbitrary and purely to illustrate the A.R.T. cycle at work.)

As the speech progresses there are many moments of potential Discovery and these allow the audience to witness the birth and development of Hamlet's Thoughts in real time, something I believe the writer intended in his, or her, use of the soliloquy.

Exercise 6.2

In a group of two or more, each person should learn a different soliloquy. Pay special attention to the Thoughts which drive each Unit. Once the Thoughts are clarified, take turns performing the speech but **without speaking the text**. The person or persons watching will see the Thought journey of the speaker as it happens. Look out for moments of Discovery and Thoughts which drive landmark Units.

When performing the Thought journey, try not to just think the text; the thoughts driving the text will be a little different. It may take time to get used to learning the Thought journey, but this is the heart of the speech, the stone which initiates the flow of ripples across the surface of the pond.

Once everyone has satisfactorily performed the Thought journey, try adding the text but make sure that the Thoughts are still present, and that they are 'driving' the text.

I have seen many deliveries of the 'To be or not to be' speech where the actor presents the text without Thought, as if this is something Hamlet has been thinking off stage and which he now 'presents' to the audience almost as if it were a lecture.

Each mode of the A.R.T. sequence is different and can be practised separately, with each lending a different dimension to the drama within a scene. Once an actor is comfortable with the system, switching between modes is automatic and the Thoughts, Actions and Responses may be improvised in the moment. The crucial factor is that the Actioning is constantly assessed and reviewed just as it is in real life, that this Response gives rise to Thought and that Thought is allowed to 'drive' the lines.

Chapter 7: Emotion

For many actors, both novice and experienced, the generation of truthful Emotion is regarded as the measure of successful acting. Audiences are often most impressed with the production of real tears in a performance; in fact, it can actually take the audience out of the moment if one person whispers to the other 'Look, she's *really* crying!' This will be because the Emotional state of an actor is taking focus away from what is actually happening between the characters on stage: the drama.

But what do we mean by Emotion? In current psychological theory, Emotions are classified into groups, and although the different lists presented by various theories will invariably include anger, sadness and joy, some of them include what many would regard as Feelings such as calmness, surprise, craving, enchantment, boredom, interest, nostalgia and awe.

There is also some debate over the exact difference between Feelings and Emotions; in modern psychology the general consensus is that Feelings are manifest internally and are consciously created in Response to experience, whereas Emotions are generated unconsciously and are manifest externally as well as internally. Feelings are private and occur predominantly within the mind; Emotions are observable by others and occur in the body as well as in the mind.

This classification is rather useful for the actor, so we will be using the following terms:

Feeling: an internal state which results from a Response/Thought interaction.

Emotion: an internal and external state which results from an Objective/Obstacle interaction.

State: a collective term for both Feelings and Emotions.

First, we will deal with Feelings. If they are private and occur only within a person, can they be seen by the audience?

Let's look again at Exercise 6.2, where the actor is experiencing a series of Thoughts which drive the lines of a speech. When the actor who has performed the Thought-journey is asked to talk about the exercise, they will often describe experiencing Feelings along with the Thoughts. Additionally, the students who observe the Thought-journey will describe seeing Feelings. This shows us that the Response-Thought part of the A.R.T cycle naturally generates Feelings, and that they are, to some degree, visible to observers.

It can be very difficult to hide Feelings, especially from those who know us well. They may seem private, but they are not.

Feelings will often drive an Objective. For example, someone who feels powerless may want to alleviate this Feeling by attaining a position of power, someone who feels unloved may pursue Objectives which make them feel loved and someone who feels threatened may seek situations in which they feel safe. These Feelings may be a fundamental part of a person's qualities (their Character) or they may result from a Response to the circumstances or drama within the scene. Since this book doesn't deal with Character, we will be looking at Feelings resulting from Response.

As part of the A.R.T cycle, when an actor observes another character's Response, the Thought that follows will often be connected with a Feeling such as 'he doesn't respect me' or 'she needs my reassurance'. This Feeling, or state, will drive the next Action. This can be clearly seen in the analysis of Hamlet's 'To be or not to be' speech in Chapter 6.

Emotions, by contrast, are usually a by-product of the interaction between an Objective and an Obstacle. For example, a person who is persistently asking for someone else to move out of the way, without success, may become angry or irritated, someone who is looking for their car keys but cannot find them may become upset or stressed, and someone who overcomes a major Obstacle, such as passing a driving test, may experience relief or joy, before deriving and tackling their next Objective. These states will often become additional Obstacles because they have physical effects which don't aid, but in fact hinder, rational dialogue.

Feelings resulting from a Response that drive an Objective are not particularly problematic for the actor; as long as the actor is truthfully invested in pursuing their Objective and looking for a Response, this will drive Thought, and a Feeling will occur naturally.

The states that often present difficulties for the actor are those that result from an Objective/Obstacle interaction, predominantly anger and sadness as well as other 'negative' states. There is a tendency for actors to focus on generating these kinds of Emotions directly; this will not produce truthful situations.

Imagine a situation where a woman is leaving her husband. They've had a disagreement and she tells him she's leaving. He is surprised (a Feeling); he doesn't really believe her. She goes upstairs to pack a bag and after a while he follows her. He watches her putting some of her things into a suitcase. He tells her that she's being silly and even though it seems more serious, he still doesn't believe she'll go. (By now he may be Feeling uneasy.) She's finished packing and she's going downstairs; he asks her to stop and talk about it, but she won't. Now he's starting to believe that she may actually leave, and he starts to plead with her. By the time she gets to the front door he's in a desperate state, begging her to stay; perhaps he has tears in his eyes. But she opens the door, picks up her case and walks through the doorway. Now he knows she is really intent on leaving and he tells her she cannot leave. Perhaps he becomes angry or breaks down in tears.

In this situation the man is not trying to generate these Emotions. His Objective is to make her decide to stay; it probably doesn't help him to cry and it certainly doesn't help him to become angry. All of his effort is focused on making his wife stay and as she gets closer to leaving, his effort increases. Once he is Emotional it becomes harder to speak coherently as more of his effort is focused on overcoming the Emotion in order to make her stay.

What is actually happening is that his Emotion is being generated as a by-product of the conflict between his Objective and the Obstacle he needs to overcome. As additional Obstacles are presented (his wife going upstairs, packing her case, going towards the door and eventually leaving the house), his effort to overcome them increases and, because he cannot overcome them, this continued effort results in Emotion. He is putting lots of energy into overcoming the Obstacle in order to achieve the Objective, but the Obstacle is not weakening, so the energy, which has to go somewhere, is forced into creating an Emotional state.

We usually become Emotional when we are trying very hard to get what we want but we are not succeeding. As we apply energy to overcoming the Obstacle, if no progress is made, and we keep applying energy, this energy builds up and will eventually lead to some kind of Emotional state.

If we give up on the Objective, we become resigned to failure, stoically accepting the situation, and with this Response the energy dissipates into a Feeling, which will now drive a new Objective.

Alternatively, we may be trying to accept failure (our Objective), attempting to overcome our pride (the Obstacle) and thereby dealing with a new Objective/Obstacle conflict; this new situation may give rise to a fresh Emotional state. Once we have accepted the failure, as in the previous paragraph, our Response to this new situation may lead to a Feeling which will drive a new Objective.

If we overcome the original Obstacle and get closer to achieving our Objective, our Response may lead to a positive Feeling of relief, excitement or elation. But it is the continued effort of pursuing an Objective in the face of an insurmountable Obstacle or Obstacles that produces a truthful Emotional state.

Exercise 7.1

Think of the last time you experienced negative Emotions. You should be able to identify an Objective which you were pursuing and an Obstacle which you were trying to overcome.

If you were involved in dialogue, you will probably recall that the Emotional state didn't help you to communicate effectively and probably didn't help you to achieve your Objective; it will have become another Obstacle to overcome.

But what does this mean for the actor? The first implication is that an actor should not aim for Emotion but rather identify the Obstacles which stand in the way of the Objective and put effort and focus into overcoming them. In terms of energy it is similar to hitting a wall with your fist; if the wall doesn't give way the energy will cause pain and damage to your hand. If the actor continues to apply energy, in terms of Actioning, to overcoming the Obstacle and it doesn't give way, the energy will produce an Emotional state.

Once this happens the actor should deal with the Emotion as an additional Obstacle; this will require further effort and often a new Emotional state will develop.

For example, someone who is becoming angry will start to tremble, they will feel an impulse to raise their voice and will possibly feel the need to take physical action in order to achieve their Objectives. If these impulses are indulged, the result will be someone shouting at the top of their voice with no physical control and possibly using violence. In actuality, the person will be trying incredibly hard to keep their voice at a reasonable volume and to inhibit the loss of control of their body; this effort will produce a new Emotional state, possibly even some kind of Emotional collapse.

We can probably all remember a very scary teacher who would never shout but spoke very slowly and quietly when they were angry; this may have been a practised tactic, but perhaps they were working to control their temper.

The Emotional states which result will often be unexpected, as in real life. The most poignant aspect of this approach is that the character will not be seen to 'indulge' in the Emotion but rather to deal with it as an additional Obstacle; their focus will be on the pursuit of their Objective and not on achieving an Emotional state.

Exercise 7.2

Actors A and B are given Objectives.

A's Objective is 'to make B say yes'.

B's Objective is 'to make A accept no as an answer'.

Within the improvisation each can invent a backstory if they wish (a reason for the 'yes' or 'no') but this should not be revealed in the dialogue. As each actor encounters a new Obstacle, they should directly tackle this Obstacle in pursuit of their Objective. It might start off like this:

A   Say yes.

B   No.

A   Come on, please?

B   No.

A   Look, this is really important to me.

B   You? What about me?

A   I know it's a big thing for you…

B   You don't know, or you wouldn't keep asking me!

A   Please, can you just do this one thing for me?

B   I've said no and that's the end of it!

A   Please just think about it.

B   I've thought about it in detail and the answer is still no.

A   You're just being selfish!

B   Me? You need to grow up and accept that no means no!

A   Please? I'm begging you…

B   Don't humiliate yourself. You're wasting your breath!

A   How can you be so cold?

B   Cold? You're like a spoilt child; you can't get what you want so you're being nasty!

A   I'm sorry…

B   Let's move on.

A   I can't!

B   Just LET IT GO! OK?

A   Let's talk about it.

B   No.

Both actors should keep to the issue of achieving their Objectives and avoid introducing unnecessary or distracting information.

When novice actors are improvising the playing of Objectives, there can be a tendency to introduce information which will compel the other actor to fulfil the Objective. For example, Actor A might say 'You said yes this morning' or 'If you say no, thousands of people will die' or even 'If you don't say yes, I'll kill myself!' In these situations, the actor is relying on information to make the other actor do what they want instead of Actioning them, using *Transitive Verbs*. The use of information in this way should be avoided; the actors should use only their ability to connect with the other person honestly and truthfully as a means to achieve their Objective.

As the improvisation is performed, other students/actors should observe how Responses result in Thoughts and Feelings. It is helpful for the observers to make a note of these Feelings as the exercise progresses.

If both actors are strictly playing their Objectives and directly attempting to tackle the Obstacles presented, Emotional states, such as anger or sorrow, will arise.

At some point actor B should say yes. This should not happen until after Emotional states have been observed or at least until the energy has built significantly; this can be determined by a prearranged discreet signal from the tutor or decided by the actor playing B.

Once Actor B has fulfilled A's Objective, the improvisation should be allowed to continue for a few moments as Feelings and Emotions such as joy, relief or excitement emerge from the new situation.

It will be clear to the observers if an actor is playing the Emotion instead of the Objective; in this instance the improvisation should be stopped, the observation shared with the actors and the rest of the group, and the exercise continued.

It may take several attempts with different actors, but eventually the exercise will demonstrate the different ways in which Feelings and Emotions are truthfully produced.

In the early parts of the exercise, Feelings will be noted as part of the actors' Response to Obstacles which are presented.

Once the energy applied to the Obstacles has built to a sufficient level, Emotional states such as anger, desperation and sorrow will arise.

Finally, when A's Objective has been achieved, positive Emotions, such as relief or joy, will be produced.

Positive States

There are two ways in which positive states will be produced.

A positive Feeling can emerge as a Response to a new situation, such as a sign that progress towards A's Objective is being made.

A positive Emotion can result if the build-up of pressure to overcome Obstacles is suddenly released when the Objective is achieved; this will occur if the investment in the Objective was of sufficient depth.

In some cases, this will be observed at the end of exercise 7.2.

This will often occur in a moment of Discovery, as mentioned in Chapter 6.

Imagine somebody is pushing with all their might to open a door which has jammed, and it suddenly opens. The energy which was focused directly at the door (the Obstacle) will now send them flying through the doorway in an unfocused, chaotic fashion as the Objective is suddenly achieved. This sudden release of energy is similar to the way in which positive Emotions are produced.

Imagine a physicist who has a sudden realisation that may solve a long-established scientific problem. Perhaps he or she has been considering this issue for years, applying mental energy towards overcoming an enduring and seemingly impenetrable Obstacle. At the moment of Discovery, the Obstacle is overcome, and the built-up energy is allowed to run free. Just as the breaking of a dam will release water to energetically find a new route towards the sea, the energy which the physicist has applied to the long-standing problem will now release Thought to surge towards new Objectives.

For the actor this will mean making a strong investment in the Objective, clearly identifying and applying energy towards overcoming the Obstacles, and allowing this energy to strongly drive new Thought following the moment of Discovery.

There are some acting techniques in which Emotion is seen as the root of Action and the Emotional state of the actor is prioritised above all else. I have worked with actors trained in some of these styles who work hard to generate Emotion, often from the recall of personal experience, before investing in the truth of the scene. This will often result in a scene, or part of a scene, which is awash with unrestrained Emotion and where the drama is played in parallel, even becoming secondary to or subverted by this Emotion.

In these cases, the words of the text can be seen to 'surf' on top of the Emotion; they lose their meaning and become part of a wave of Emotional release. Although this may impress some audiences, directors and actors, it bears little relationship to the way in which Emotion interacts with text and dramatic situations in the real world.

If the actor's attention is focused on generating an Emotional state, the audience will see this and the level of truth will be diminished.

Exceptions

There will of course be situations when a person, or character, is using their Emotional state to get what they want; they are 'faking it'. This should be a choice for the actor and the result will be understandably and desirably different from the more truthful Objective/Obstacle conflict approach.

For example, in *A Streetcar Named Desire*, some actors playing Blanche DuBois may interpret her actions as 'faking' an Emotional state in order to manipulate those around her into achieving her Objectives.

Practical Application

We have looked at how the release of the diaphragm will allow the central nervous system to affect the voice and body. When using Objective/Obstacle conflict to allow Emotional states to be generated, it is important for the actor to maintain a free diaphragm. This will allow any Emotional states to be fully embodied in their expression.

There is of course the potential for a character to be 'Emotionally Bound', holding tension in their diaphragm as a way to suppress their Emotion; again, this should be a choice made by the actor.

There are many different options for the actor using this approach. When an apparently insurmountable Obstacle is tackled, *Transitive Verbs* may be changed rapidly, for example *Implore – Command – Threaten – Entreat – Condemn. Abstract Transitive Verbs* may also be considered.

An actor might consider switching from an external Obstacle (presented by the other person) to an internal Obstacle (within their own character).

The Objective itself may be changed in order to make it harder to achieve, resulting in more excess energy with no escape route except the production of Emotion.

When somebody is struggling with Emotion, desperately trying *not* to cry, for example, it will be very moving for members of those watching.

Imagine a situation in which a small child has been bullied. They come to tell a parent what happened, and they are bravely trying not to cry as they struggle with the words. For the parent this will be heart-rending; they can feel the conflict within the child and can sense the suppressed river of Emotion. But once they pick the child up and the child can safely cry in the arms of their parent, relief is felt by both.

The build-up to Emotional release often carries conflict and will produce tension in the audience. Imagine watching a scene where you know that A is angry with B and you can see that A is working really hard to suppress the rage within. It is the audience that will feel the pressure and tension of this suppressed rage; the audience will be anticipating the dreadful moment of release.

With sadness it is the same: if a character is bravely fighting the impulse to cry, the audience will see this, they will feel the pressure of this impulse and it is consequently more likely that the audience will be the ones who shed tears. They will be real, honest and very truthful tears, created by the actor but realised in the eyes of the audience.

Example of Emotion Produced in a Scene

In the following scene from *A Doll's House* there are sections where the conflict between Objective and Obstacle within a character might generate an Emotional state.

Nora's Overall Objective is clearly 'to get Helmer to reverse his decision to dismiss Krogstad'; she plays this Objective until Unit 18, when she concludes that this Objective is no longer achievable. For the last two Units Nora is reviewing her situation, possibly in a state of shock, and her Objective at this point will depend greatly on interpretation of the impact of Krogstad's dismissal letter having been sent; it might be something like 'to get her husband ready for the forthcoming changes to their life together'.

Helmer's Objective for the first two Units might be 'to get Nora to be open and clear with him' but for most of the scene it seems to be 'to get Nora to accept that Krogstad must be dismissed'; his Objective for the last two Units seems to be 'to get Nora to accept his authority as leader'. This Objective will also encompass the previous two Objectives: 'to get Nora to be open and clear with him' and 'to get Nora to accept that Krogstad must be dismissed'. It may be more useful to use this Objective throughout the entire scene although each individual Unit Objective will be more specific and will form a step towards this Overall Objective.

The choices regarding Unit divisions and Objective/Obstacle have been made purely for this example and are to some degree subjective and arbitrary; different actors and directors will make substantially different choices. The important point is that choices are made and that Objectives at a smaller scale contribute to Objectives at a larger scale.

The first two Units are started by Nora; Helmer seems to be calmly trying to maintain control.

UNIT 1

NORA. Torvald.

HELMER. Yes

NORA. If your little squirrel were to ask you for something very, very prettily—?

HELMER. What then?

NORA. Would you do it?

HELMER. I should like to hear what it is, first.

UNIT 2

NORA. Your squirrel would run about and do all her tricks if you would be nice, and do what she wants.

HELMER. Speak plainly.

NORA. Your skylark would chirp about in every room, with her song rising and falling—

HELMER. Well, my skylark does that anyhow.

NORA. I would play the fairy and dance for you in the moonlight, Torvald.

Unit 3 is started by Helmer when he realises the nature of Nora's request. He has already spoken to Nora about this so, in terms of his Objective 'to get Nora to accept his authority as leader', his discovery of Nora's request presents a new Obstacle; this will lead to his Objective being played with greater force.

UNIT 3

HELMER. Nora—you surely don't mean that request you made to me this morning?

NORA. [Going near him] Yes, Torvald, I beg you so earnestly—

HELMER. Have you really the courage to open up that question again?

NORA. Yes, dear, you must do as I ask; you must let Krogstad keep his post in the bank.

In Unit 4 Helmer seems to believe he has found a perfect way to achieve his Objective, with few or no Obstacles to overcome; as a result, he may play his Objective with a lower level of effort.

UNIT 4

HELMER. My dear Nora, it is his post that I have arranged Mrs Linde shall have.

NORA. Yes, you have been awfully kind about that; but you could just as well dismiss some other clerk instead of Krogstad.

At the end of Unit 4 Nora gives Helmer direct advice concerning his management of the bank. This presents a new and considerable Obstacle to his Objective; it is reflected in the intensity with which he plays his Objective in Unit 5.

UNIT 5

HELMER. This is simply incredible obstinacy! Because you chose to give him a thoughtless promise that you would speak for him, I am expected to—

NORA. That isn't the reason, Torvald. It is for your own sake. This fellow writes in the most scurrilous newspapers; you have told me so yourself. He can do you an unspeakable amount of harm. I am frightened to death of him—

In Unit 6 Helmer believes he has identified the nature of the Obstacle to be Nora's fear that he will suffer in the same way as her father did; this leads to a more compassionate playing of his Objective. He believes this Obstacle will be easily overcome.

UNIT 6

HELMER. Ah, I understand; it is recollections of the past that scare you.

NORA. What do you mean?

HELMER. Naturally you are thinking of your father.

NORA. Yes—yes, of course.

In Unit 7 Nora capitalises on Helmer's misinterpretation of her motive, using his potential loss of reputation and accordingly his loss of income as the apparent driver for her Objective.

UNIT 7

NORA (continued).   Just recall to your mind what these malicious creatures wrote in the papers about papa, and how horribly they slandered him. I believe they would have procured his dismissal if the Department had not sent you over to inquire into it, and if you had not been so kindly disposed and helpful to him.

HELMER. My little Nora, there is an important difference between your father and me. Your father's reputation as a public official was not above suspicion. Mine is, and I hope it will continue to be so, as long as I hold my office.

NORA. You never can tell what mischief these men may contrive. We ought to be so well off, so snug and happy here in our peaceful home, and have no cares—you and I and the children, Torvald! That is why I beg you so earnestly—

In Units 8 and 9 Helmer is becoming exasperated with his wife's relentless pursuit of her Objective so he states that her attempt to intercede is the very reason why he must dismiss Krogstad. He believes that this will be 'check mate' but Nora counters each attempt Helmer makes to overcome every Obstacle presented. This causes a continual increase in the pressure Helmer is applying to overcome Obstacles; this excess energy may well lead to Emotion.

UNIT 8

HELMER. And it is just by interceding for him that you make it impossible for me to keep him. It is already known at the Bank that I mean to dismiss Krogstad. Is it to get about now that the new manager has changed his mind at his wife's bidding—

NORA. And what if it did?

UNIT 9

HELMER. Of course!—if only this obstinate little person can get her way! Do you suppose I am going to make myself ridiculous before my whole staff, to let people think that I am a man to be swayed by all sorts of outside influence? I should very soon feel the consequences of it, I can tell you!

In Units 10, 11 and 12 Helmer starts to introduce the idea that it is actually Krogstad's air of familiarity with him in front of his colleagues that bothers him most. He is now presenting an almost insurmountable Obstacle to Nora.

UNIT 10

HELMER (continued). And besides, there is one thing that makes it quite impossible for me to have Krogstad in the Bank as long as I am manager.

NORA. Whatever is that?

UNIT 11

+HELMER. His moral failings I might perhaps have overlooked, if necessary—

NORA. Yes, you could—couldn't you?

HELMER. And I hear he is a good worker, too.

UNIT 12

HELMER (continued). But I knew him when we were boys. It was one of those rash friendships that so often prove an incubus in afterlife. I may as well tell you plainly, we were once on very intimate terms with one another. But this tactless fellow lays no restraint on himself when other people are present. On the contrary, he thinks it gives him the right to adopt a familiar tone with me, and every minute it is "I say, Helmer, old fellow!" and that sort of thing. I assure you it is extremely painful for me. He would make my position in the Bank intolerable.

This is a difficult Obstacle for Nora to overcome so she resorts to calling him 'narrow-minded' in Unit 13.

UNIT 13

NORA. Torvald, I don't believe you mean that.

HELMER. Don't you? Why not?

NORA. Because it is such a narrow-minded way of looking at things.

HELMER. What are you saying? Narrow-minded? Do you think I am narrow-minded?

NORA. No, just the opposite, dear—and it is exactly for that reason.

HELMER. It's the same thing. You say my point of view is narrow-minded, so I must be so too. Narrow-minded!

This has proved too offensive to Helmer so in Unit 14 he impetuously arranges for the dismissal letter to be sent straight away. (Nora has actually identified an Obstacle to Helmer's Objective which is internal, i.e. it is inside Helmer: his own belief that he may be considered to be narrow-minded.) He is attempting to achieve his Objective with great force and although he enforces his command, he does not get his wife's agreement so his Objective ('To get Nora to accept is authority as leader') has not been

achieved. His continued effort to achieve his Objective will probably lead to some kind of Emotional state.

In this and the next Unit Nora sees a new and unidentified Obstacle being placed in the way of her Objective; this will lead to greater effort to achieve her Objective.

UNIT 14

HELMER (continued). Very well—I must put an end to this. [Goes to the hall door and calls] Helen!

NORA. What are you going to do?

HELMER. [Looking among his papers] Settle it.

UNIT 15

[Enter MAID]

HELMER (continued). Look here; take this letter and go downstairs with it at once. Find a messenger and tell him to deliver it, and be quick. The address is on it, and here is the money.

MAID. Very well, sir. [Exits with the letter]

In Unit 16 Helmer tries to get his wife to accept his authority by force; he has used his power and wishes to see

her accept this. Nora realises what is in the letter but her need to achieve her Objective makes her seek confirmation; her hope, against the Obstacle of virtual certainty, is played with desperate force. This will probably result in an Emotional state.

UNIT 16

HELMER. [Putting his papers together] Now then, little Miss Obstinate.

NORA. [Breathlessly] Torvald—what was that letter?

HELMER. Krogstad's dismissal.

In Unit 17 the only way she can achieve her Objective is to have the letter stopped before it is delivered. Her Obstacle now is her husband's stubbornness, his belief in his absolute authority and to some degree the internal Obstacle of her gender-based confidence. She does not abandon her Objective, even though the Obstacles are virtually insurmountable, and this will almost certainly lead to some kind of Emotion.

UNIT 17

NORA. Call her back, Torvald! There is still time. Oh Torvald, call her back! Do it for my sake—for your own sake—for the children's sake! Do you hear me, Torvald? Call her back! You don't know what that letter can bring upon us.

HELMER. It's too late.

In Unit 18 her state has become calm; this is because she has given up the Objective 'to get Helmer to reconsider his decision to dismiss Krogstad' in favour of a new, more relevant Objective. As stated above this might be something like 'to get her husband to prepare for the forthcoming changes to their life together'. If the line in this Unit is delivered to herself, instead of to Helmer, the Objective might be 'to prepare herself for the forthcoming changes to her life'.

Helmer, seeing the drastic change to Nora, still plays his Objective but he does so with compassion, albeit of a patronising nature.

UNIT 18

NORA. Yes, it's too late.

HELMER. My dear Nora, I can forgive the anxiety you are in, although really it is an insult to me. It is, indeed. Isn't it an insult to think that I should be afraid of a starving quill-driver's vengeance? But I forgive you nevertheless, because it is such eloquent witness to your great love for me.

UNIT 19

HELMER (continued). [Takes her in his arms] And that is as it should be, my own darling Nora. Come what will, you may be sure I shall have both courage and strength if they be needed. You will see I am man enough to take everything upon myself.

NORA. [In a horror-stricken voice] What do you mean by that?

HELMER. Everything, I say—

NORA. [Recovering herself] You will never have to do that.

Chapter 8: Truthful Physical Expression

One of the most common issues facing novice actors is 'I don't know what to do with my hands!' When someone starts acting, their awareness of their own body can seem overwhelming by comparison to their day-to-day existence, in which their body behaves naturally and they rarely even notice it.

This is a symptom of the actor's focus and attention being on themselves rather than on the person or people they're trying to affect in order to achieve their Objective. This awareness is disproportionately focused on their body, which can make them feel physically awkward and will stifle any expressive impulses.

In the early stages of an actor's development, this issue is often 'dealt with' by the actor being encouraged to stand still and to avoid using their hands and arms. Although this may diminish the unwanted awkwardness of physical self-awareness, it will entirely rule out the potential for free and truthful physical expression.

Once an actor is familiar with the concept of Objective pursuit through Actioning, they will be focusing almost entirely on the other person and they should start to feel impulses to engage physically with the forces which are driving them psychologically. I often see actors at this stage feeling an impulse to move but rejecting it as a result of earlier, more basic training, which has discouraged the free rein of physical expression. This will often be seen as a twitch or a half step in some direction, or perhaps one hand is moving a little, along with the progress of the text.

Novice actors, given the option, will often make the choice to sit rather than stand while performing; this will feel 'safer' as the body, in a sitting position, is relatively immobile from the neck down so the physical awkwardness felt in the standing position, when the body is free to move, is no longer present.

This means that the actor is not learning how to 'use' the rest of their body truthfully; once they are directed to stand, walk or involve their character in some physical Action, their attention will be drawn to this new and hitherto unexplored area of themselves.

So how may an actor solve this problem?

Stand Up

The first step in resolving this problem will be to stand up while acting at every opportunity, especially when training. If the script doesn't explicitly state that the character should be sitting, or the director hasn't requested that the actor should sit, then the actor should stand in order to allow this extra dimension to become available and be explored. The option to sit will always be there if a chair, table or other structure is available; this may be used at a poignant moment or to make a specific point or statement about the character or the drama within the scene, perhaps even as the result of a natural impulse.

The option to fully utilise the performance space will allow the actor to explore the character's use of, and their relationship with, the space around them. Choices and discoveries may be made regarding myriad parameters governing a character's movement, many of which would be unavailable if the character were sitting down.

Once these parameters have been discovered they may be applied to the character while seated, but their Discovery will be more difficult and less likely if the character is not allowed the freedom to use their body and the space around them in the early, developmental phase.

Action Without Words

When the text is removed from a situation, the Objectives, Obstacles and Actions will still be present, relevant and available for exploration. Without the crutch of the text the relationship between different characters, and between each character and the performance space, may be explored fully.

The text, being the primary structure of the script, will often dominate all major aspects of any performance. If we find ways to explore the structure without this dominance, the characters' physicality has the freedom to take on a more fundamental role.

As mentioned in Chapter 4 on Advanced Actioning, The Shop Game may be played with no text: an actor will enter the shop with a *Transitive Verb* in mind and apply this to the shopkeeper using just eye contact and their body within the space. They should walk into the shop applying the *Transitive Verb* and then stand at the counter still applying the *Transitive Verb* to the shopkeeper.

When actors first attempt the Shop Game without words, there can be a tendency to mime, signal or physicalise in an exaggerated or untruthful way, in order that the *Transitive Verb* in question is guessed by the onlookers.

This should be noted, either by the actors themselves or those observing, and truthful physical expression encouraged.

When an actor behaves in a physically unnatural way, they, and the audience, can feel it; an example might be when someone is 'off-centre', when they are leaning forwards or to one side, when they are not 'grounded'.

Exercise 8.1

Improvise a door-to-door salesperson selling The World's Best *Something*. Initially start the sales routine with all of your weight on one leg, an 'ungrounded' stance.

Then do the same sales routine but with your feet a shoulder's width apart, in a firmly grounded stance.

Ask the observers to judge which salesperson will be believed and trusted more.

You should notice a marked difference in the level of truth between the two versions.

We often use *Transitive Verbs* without text in our daily lives in order to pursue Objectives; perhaps in a public situation we may not mention an issue which we are dealing with but the person who we are Actioning will know that they are being confronted, challenged, appeased or mocked by our expression along with our body language.

In this situation it is our focus on the other person and our intention to make them feel something and as a result, to *DO* or *SAY* something (our Objective) which will allow our body to behave naturally and to 'speak' with truth.

When rehearsing a scene it is useful for the actors to attempt to play their Objectives without words, just using their bodies and the space, before starting to work with the text.

It is also useful to allow actors to improvise, without words, situations where an Obstacle is not overcome. For example, if a character is overcoming an internal Obstacle of anger, it may be useful to explore what happens physically if the anger is not overcome and is allowed to reign free for a few minutes. This will give the actor a real sense of what they are trying to avoid in overcoming the Obstacle, a sense of the possible outcome if the Actioning, or the resistance to an internal Obstacle, is not in some way successful.

It can also be useful for an actor to explore their physical reaction to achieving a difficult Objective. For example, the character may want a hug from another character, their mother for example; if they improvise this hug 'in character' before the scene then both actors will have an idea of how this possible outcome feels, and the feeling of not getting the hug in the actual performed scene may be more poignant for both of them.

Follow Impulses

An actor in training should get in the habit of following impulses as they arise; anything which is not deemed to be useful or truthful can be deselected for performance, but it is always better to have too much to choose from than not enough. The rehearsal room should be seen as a safe place to follow impulses without the pressure of entertaining an audience.

A director will find it easier to ask an actor to do less of something than to try to drag something out of an actor which is not present.

We experience different kinds of impulses in each of the three modes: Action, Response and Thought.

When we are Actioning, our bodies are intimately connected to our words, and together they are trying to make somebody else feel something. As we are speaking, our diaphragm is attempting to exert the right pressure to make each word work as effectively as possible, and the Action of the diaphragm can be seen, and felt, in the entire body.

When we are looking for Response, and responding to the Response we see, we usually release our diaphragm; this also has a significant physical effect which can be seen and felt. Additionally, a released diaphragm will allow the body to express more of what the actor, or the character, feels.

When we are thinking, we will not only 'feed' our brain with oxygen by breathing deeply, reflected in the diaphragm and hence the rest of the body, but also allow our attention to drift from the actual space of the scene into Thought-space, also seen and felt in the body.

It has already been mentioned that an actor may improvise playing an Objective by Actioning without words and this can also be applied to Response; an actor can focus on the Response of another character and explore this in purely physical terms.

The benefit of this exercise is most profoundly seen when physical improvisation of a Thought process is explored, as below.

Exercise 8.2

Using a monologue in which you've clearly identified the Thoughts which drive each Unit, allow yourself to use the space freely and act upon all physical impulses while following the Thought journey. There should be no text and the actor should be thinking the Thoughts, not the lines, which drive the text. There will be clear differences between problems, decisions and discoveries, all different kinds of Thought. You will see how breath, the energy powerhouse of the brain, drives Thought and how this will breed impulses to shape and move the body within the space.

Impulse is what makes our bodies express truth in real life, so we should allow impulse to play its part in our expression as actors.

When practising these techniques to allow truthful physical expression, the actor will often discover ways of moving which are not natural, truthful or useful; usually this will be immediately obvious as it will feel 'wrong'. Over time these moments will become fewer as the actor learns to allow and trust all impulses which lead to truthful physical expression.

Chapter 9: Text Analysis Example

The following scene has been divided into Units with Objectives and Obstacles for each character. The Unit divisions along with the Objectives and Obstacles are subjective and to some degree arbitrary; different actors and directors will make different choices. This is not intended to be a definitive analysis of the scene or characters; it merely represents one in a virtually infinite number of possible interpretations.

UNIT	Krogstad's Unit Objective and **Obstacle**	Nora's Unit Objective and **Obstacle**
UNIT 1 [Meanwhile there has been a knock at the hall door, but none of them has noticed it. The door is half opened, and KROGSTAD appears, he waits a little; the game goes on.] KROGSTAD. Excuse me, Mrs Helmer.	To get Nora to accept the legitimacy of his uninvited presence in her home **He has entered uninvited; it is not legitimate**	To make Krogstad acknowledge that he should not have come in **She is scared of him**

NORA. [With a stifled cry, turns round and gets up on to her knees] Ah! what do you want? KROGSTAD. Excuse me, the outer door was ajar; I suppose someone forgot to shut it.		
UNIT 2 NORA. [Rising] My husband is out, Mr Krogstad. KROGSTAD. I know that.	To make Nora accept that she must deal with him alone **She can insist that he leaves**	To make Krogstad confirm that it is not appropriate for him to be alone with her in her home **She knows that she is in his debt and therefore under his power**
UNIT 3 NORA. What do you want here, then? KROGSTAD. A word with you.	To get Nora to be prepared to engage openly with him	To make him confirm that his visit does not concern any threat to her security

NORA. With me?—	**Her fear of him**	**His very presence threatens her security**
UNIT 4 [To the children, gently] Go in to nurse. What? No, the strange man won't do mother any harm. When he has gone we will have another game. [She takes the children into the room on the left, and shuts the door after them]	To get Nora to see and treat him as a reasonable man (i.e. he remains silent and doesn't disturb her relationship with her children) **His uninvited entry was not reasonable**	To make the children leave the room without becoming alarmed **She is flustered and the children might notice this**
UNIT 5 NORA. You want to speak to me? KROGSTAD. Yes, I do.	To make her focus on what he says **She is flustered**	To make him accept that she is not afraid of him and thereby stop trying to intimidate her **She is afraid of him**

UNIT 6 NORA. Today? It is not the first of the month yet. KROGSTAD. No, it is Christmas Eve, and it will depend on yourself what sort of a Christmas you will spend. NORA. What do you mean? Today it is absolutely impossible for me— KROGSTAD. We won't talk about that until later on.	To make Nora realise the importance of the forthcoming conversation and to respond accordingly by allowing him to take control **She doesn't know why he needs to speak to her**	To make Krogstad stop troubling her and leave **The status difference between them; in terms of the secret loan and their respective genders**
UNIT 7 KROGSTAD. This is something different. I presume you can give me a moment?	To make her listen with an open mind	To make him acknowledge her compromise in allowing the forthcoming conversation

NORA. Yes—yes, I can—although— KROGSTAD. Good.	**She is not comfortable speaking to him secretly within her home**	**She feels she has no choice but to allow him to speak**
UNIT 8 I was in Olsen's Restaurant and saw your husband going down the street— NORA. Yes? KROGSTAD. With a lady.	To get Nora to confirm that Mrs Linde is in town	To satisfy Krogstad so that he will leave
NORA. What then? KROGSTAD. May I make so bold as to ask if it was a Mrs Linde? NORA. It was. KROGSTAD. Just arrived in town?	**He believes that they have conspired against him so she may try to withhold the information**	**She doesn't know exactly what he wants**

NORA. Yes, today.		
UNIT 9 KROGSTAD. She is a great friend of yours, isn't she? NORA. She is. But I don't see— KROGSTAD. I knew her too, once upon a time. NORA. I am aware of that. KROGSTAD. Are you? So you know all about it; I thought as much.	To make Nora admit her prior knowledge of the relationship between himself and Mrs Linde **He isn't certain that she has knowledge of this**	To make him explain his motives for asking about Mrs Linde **He is clearly in control of the conversation**
UNIT 10 KROGSTAD. Then I can ask you, without beating about the bush—is Mrs Linde to have an appointment in the Bank?	To make her confirm that he is being dismissed in favour of Mrs Linde	To make him acknowledge her status and power with regard to the bank

NORA. What right have you to question me, Mr Krogstad?—You, one of my husband's subordinates! But since you ask, you shall know. Yes, Mrs Linde is to have an appointment. And it was I who pleaded her cause, Mr Krogstad, let me tell you that. KROGSTAD. I was right in what I thought, then.	**He assumes she will be reluctant to reveal that she has been instrumental in his dismissal**	**He has gender status and power over her due to the loan**
UNIT 11 NORA. [Walking up and down the stage] Sometimes one has a tiny little bit of influence, I should hope. Because one is a woman, it does not necessarily follow that—.	To make Nora confirm her power with respect to the bank	To make Krogstad respect and fear her

When anyone is in a subordinate position, Mr Krogstad, they should really be careful to avoid offending anyone who—who— KROGSTAD. Who has influence? NORA. Exactly.	**She may realise his trap**	**He has had power over her for a long time due to the loan**
UNIT 12 KROGSTAD. [Changing his tone] Mrs Helmer, you will be so good as to use your influence on my behalf.	To make her agree to persuade her husband to keep him in his job	To make him tell her why he needs her help
NORA. What? What do you mean?	**He knows that she is subservient to her husband**	**He is intent only on getting her assurance that she will help him**
KROGSTAD. You will be so kind as to see that I am allowed to keep my		

subordinate position in the Bank. NORA. What do you mean by that? Who proposes to take your post away from you?		
UNIT 13 KROGSTAD. Oh, there is no necessity to keep up the pretence of ignorance. I can quite understand that your friend is not very anxious to expose herself to the chance of rubbing shoulders with me; and I quite understand, too, whom I have to thank for being turned off. NORA. But I assure you— KROGSTAD. Very likely; but, to	To make her admit that she was instrumental in him being replaced by Mrs Linde at the bank and to get her to undo this **He believes she is being deceitful**	To get him to accept that she had no idea he was to be dismissed **He is convinced that she was involved in instigating his dismissal**

come to the point, the time has come when I should advise you to use your influence to prevent that.		
UNIT 14 NORA. But, Mr Krogstad, I have no influence.	To get her to admit that she can influence her husband's decisions	To get him to acknowledge that her influence is minimal
KROGSTAD. Haven't you? I thought you said yourself just now—		
NORA. Naturally I did not mean you to put that construction on it. I! What should make you think I have any influence of that kind with my husband?	**Her reluctance to help him**	**She has just boasted that she has influence**
KROGSTAD. Oh, I have known your husband from our student days. I don't suppose he is any more		

unassailable than other husbands.		
UNIT 15 NORA. If you speak slightingly of my husband, I shall turn you out of the house.	To make her question herself by showing his confidence in the face of her threat	To make him apologise for making this remark about Helmer
KROGSTAD. You are bold, Mrs Helmer.	**She doesn't see the danger she is in**	**Her gender and his power over her**
UNIT 16 NORA. I am not afraid of you any longer. As soon as the New Year comes, I shall in a very short time be free of the whole thing. KROGSTAD. [Controlling himself] Listen to me, Mrs Helmer. If necessary, I am prepared to fight for	To make her back down and show him some respect **Her determination**	To make him back down and retract his request for intervention **His determination**

my small post in the Bank as if I were fighting for my life. NORA. So it seems.		
UNIT 17 KROGSTAD. It is not only for the sake of the money; indeed, that weighs least with me in the matter. There is another reason—well, I may as well tell you. My position is this. I daresay you know, like everybody else, that once, many years ago, I was guilty of an indiscretion. NORA. I think I have heard something of the kind. KROGSTAD. The matter never came into court; but	To get her to show him some sympathy and understanding **He has been intimidating her**	To get him to treat her as someone who is not naive **She feels that she is naive by comparison to him**

109

every way seemed to be closed to me after that. So I took to the business that you know of. I had to do something; and, honestly, I don't think I've been one of the worst. But now I must cut myself free from all that. My sons are growing up; for their sake I must try and win back as much respect as I can in the town. This post in the Bank was like the first step up for me—and now your husband is going to kick me downstairs again into the mud.		
UNIT 18 NORA. But you must believe me, Mr Krogstad; it is not	To make her admit that she does not want to help him	To make him accept that his efforts to enlist her help are futile

in my power to help you at all. KROGSTAD. Then it is because you haven't the will;	**Her reluctance to be truly honest with him**	**He is desperate**
UNIT 19 but I have means to compel you. NORA. You don't mean that you will tell my husband that I owe you money?	To make her accept that she has no choice **Her stubbornness**	To get him to rule out the possibility of telling Helmer **That may be his only option**
UNIT 20 KROGSTAD. Hm!—suppose I were to tell him? NORA. It would be perfectly infamous of you. [Sobbing] To think of his learning my secret, which has been my joy and pride, in such	To make her engage with the possibility of Helmer finding out about the loan and to consider the direness of the consequences	To make Krogstad feel sympathy for her and thereby retract his threat

an ugly, clumsy way—that he should learn it from you! And it would put me in a horribly disagreeable position— KROGSTAD. Only disagreeable?	**She may be too scared to consider this**	**He seems to be ruthless**
UNIT 21 NORA. [Impetuously] Well, do it, then!—and it will be the worse for you. My husband will see for himself what a blackguard you are, and you certainly won't keep your post then. KROGSTAD. I asked you if it was only a disagreeable scene at home that you were afraid of? NORA. If my husband does get to know of it, of	To make Nora fully consider the consequences of her actions being revealed and thereby to agree to help him **She doesn't understand the full implications of the fraud she has committed**	To make Krogstad realise the repercussions of his proposed actions and to retract the threat **Her husband may find out about the loan and she does not want this to happen**

course he will at once pay you what is still owing, and we shall have nothing more to do with you.		
UNIT 22 KROGSTAD. [Coming a step nearer] Listen to me, Mrs Helmer. Either you have a very bad memory or you know very little of business. I shall be obliged to remind you of a few details. NORA. What do you mean? KROGSTAD. When your husband was ill, you came to me to borrow two hundred and fifty pounds. NORA. I didn't know	To make her remember and confirm the exact details of the loan **She is flustered and has difficulty seeing fault in her actions**	To make him accept that she is fully acquainted with the facts and thereby stop intimidating her **He seems to be convinced that she is ignorant of some details**

anyone else to go to.

KROGSTAD.
I promised to get you that amount—

NORA.
Yes, and you did so.

KROGSTAD.
I promised to get you that amount, on certain conditions. Your mind was so taken up with your husband's illness, and you were so anxious to get the money for your journey, that you seem to have paid no attention to the conditions of our bargain. Therefore it will not be amiss if I remind you of them.

Unit 23 Now, I promised to get the money on the security of a bond which I drew up. NORA. Yes, and which I signed. KROGSTAD. Good. But below your signature there were a few lines constituting your father a surety for the money; those lines your father should have signed. NORA. Should? He did sign them.	To make Nora realise that her forgery has been noted **She believes that the fraudulent signature has gone unnoticed**	To make Krogstad believe that no forgery took place **She knows that she has committed forgery**
UNIT 24 KROGSTAD. I had left the date blank; that is to say, your father should himself have inserted the date on	To get her to clearly confirm the series of events	To make him believe that she is aware of no inconsistencies in the signing of the contract

which he signed the paper. Do you remember that? NORA. Yes, I think I remember— KROGSTAD. Then I gave you the bond to send by post to your father. Is that not so? NORA. Yes. KROGSTAD. And you naturally did so at once, because five or six days afterwards you brought me the bond with your father's signature. And then I gave you the money.	**She has paid little attention to these details for years**	**She knows that she forged her father's signature**
UNIT 25 NORA. Well, haven't I been paying it off regularly?	To make her realise that repayment is not the issue	To get him to accept that the terms of the loan have been observed in spite

116

KROGSTAD. Fairly so, yes.	**She is desperate and unfocused**	of any technical issues **He is focused on a different issue**
UNIT 26 But—to come back to the matter in hand—that must have been a very trying time for you, Mrs Helmer? NORA. It was, indeed. KROGSTAD. Your father was very ill, wasn't he? NORA. He was very near his end. KROGSTAD. And died soon afterwards? NORA. Yes.	To make her respond with vulnerable honesty **She is being defensive**	To make him show sympathy and understanding **She knows she is being manipulated**

UNIT 27	Wants to make her realise that she is trapped and fully under his power	Wants him to believe that she is ignorant with regard to the problem
KROGSTAD. Tell me, Mrs Helmer, can you by any chance remember what day your father died?— on what day of the month, I mean.		
NORA. Papa died on the 29th of September.	**She won't want to admit to the fraud**	**He seems to know what she has done**
KROGSTAD. That is correct; I have ascertained it for myself. And, as that is so, there is a discrepancy [Taking a paper from his pocket] which I cannot account for.		
NORA. What discrepancy? I don't know—		
KROGSTAD. The discrepancy consists, Mrs Helmer, in the fact that your father signed this bond		

three days after his death. NORA. What do you mean? I don't understand— KROGSTAD. Your father died on the 29th of September. But, look here; your father has dated his signature the 2nd of October. It is a discrepancy, isn't it? [NORA is silent] Can you explain it to me? [NORA is still silent]		
UNIT 28 It is a remarkable thing, too, that the words "2nd of October," as well as the year, are not written in your father's handwriting	To make her realise that the date is not the issue and thereby to make her flustered	To allow him to come to a conclusion which does not incriminate her

but in one that I think I know. Well, of course it can be explained; your father may have forgotten to date his signature, and someone else may have dated it haphazard before they knew of his death. There is no harm in that.	**She is confused**	**She knows she is guilty**
UNIT 29 It all depends on the signature of the name; and that is genuine, I suppose, Mrs Helmer? It was your father himself who signed his name here?	To make her focus entirely on the forged signature and through her vulnerability to thereby admit her guilt **She is maintaining silence**	To make him accept her silence as confirmation of his stated facts **She is struggling to maintain her silence**
UNIT 30 NORA. [After a short pause, throws her head up and looks defiantly at him] No, it was	To allow her to freely admit her guilt **She may stay silent**	To make him feel that she is in control **She feels helpless**

not. It was I that wrote papa's name.		
UNIT 31 KROGSTAD. Are you aware that is a dangerous confession? NORA. In what way? You shall have your money soon.	To make her realise the danger she is in and therefore to do as he wishes **She still believes that as long as the debt is repaid, she will be free from his power**	To get him to stop threatening her **His confidence**
UNIT 32 KROGSTAD. Let me ask you a question; why did you not send the paper to your father? NORA. It was impossible; papa was so ill. If I had asked him for his signature, I should have had to tell him what the money was to be used for; and when	To make her feel regretful, helpless and in need of his reassurance **She believes that she has ultimately behaved with honour**	To make him show that he understands her motives **He has no sympathy for her**

he was so ill himself I couldn't tell him that my husband's life was in danger—it was impossible.		
UNIT 33 KROGSTAD. It would have been better for you if you had given up your trip abroad. NORA. No, that was impossible. That trip was to save my husband's life; I couldn't give that up. KROGSTAD. But did it never occur to you that you were committing a fraud on me? NORA. I couldn't take that into account; I didn't trouble	To get Nora to acknowledge the serious nature of her crime and admit that it could have been avoided **She believes she had no choice**	To get Krogstad to agree that it was unavoidable **She knows that it was a bad decision**

myself about you at all. I couldn't bear you, because you put so many heartless difficulties in my way, although you knew what a dangerous condition my husband was in.		
UNIT 34 KROGSTAD. Mrs Helmer, you evidently do not realise clearly what it is that you have been guilty of. But I can assure you that my one false step, which lost me all my reputation, was nothing more or nothing worse than what you have done. NORA. You?	To make her see herself as a criminal **She sees herself as morally superior to him**	To make him deny that he and her are on the same level **She is beginning to realise that they have both committed fraud**

UNIT 35 Do you ask me to believe that you were brave enough to run a risk to save your wife's life? KROGSTAD. The law cares nothing about motives. NORA. Then it must be a very foolish law.	To make her accept that her motives are not grounds for defence **Her lack of legal training**	To make him state that he is less virtuous than her and to denounce the law **Her lack of legal training**
UNIT 36 KROGSTAD. Foolish or not, it is the law by which you will be judged, if I produce this paper in court. NORA. I don't believe it. Is a daughter not to be allowed to spare her dying father anxiety and care? Is a wife not to be allowed to	To make her confront her dilemma squarely and choose to help him **She is still reluctant to judge her actions as immoral**	To make him agree that a virtuous motive absolves a crime **He is being practical and not allowing emotion to cloud his thought**

save her husband's life?		
UNIT 37 I don't know much about law; but I am certain that there must be laws permitting such things as that. Have you no knowledge of such laws—you who are a lawyer?	To allow her to realise and acknowledge that the law will not support her actions **Her arrogance**	To get him to confirm that the law must in some way support her position **Her lack of legal knowledge**
UNIT 38 You must be a very poor lawyer, Mr Krogstad. KROGSTAD. Maybe. But matters of business—such business as you and I have had together—do you think I don't understand that?	To make her respect his business expertise **Her lack of respect for him**	To make him question his own position regarding the legality of her forgery **His confidence**

UNIT 39 Very well. Do as you please. But let me tell you this—if I lose my position a second time, you shall lose yours with me. [He bows, and goes out through the hall]	To make her feel threatened and therefore to think seriously about her position and help him **Her stubbornness**	To make him leave without her agreement to assist him **His determination**
UNIT 40 NORA. [Appears buried in thought for a short time, then tosses her head] Nonsense! Trying to frighten me like that!—I am not so silly as he thinks. [Begins to busy herself putting the children's things in order]		To make herself feel more secure and less vulnerable **She knows she is at Krogstad's mercy**

Unit 41 And yet—?		To make herself consider the possible implications of his threat **She doesn't want to believe that his threat has weight**
UNIT 42 No, it's impossible! I did it for love's sake.		To make herself believe that all will be well **She fears that all is not well**

Chapter 10: Alternative Interpretations

The following examples show two different interpretations of the same section of text. Each version has a different set of Objectives and gives a choice of two alternative *Transitive Verbs* which may be used as a means of achieving the same Objective. There are, of course, many more *Transitive Verbs* and Objectives which may be used; the aim of this example is to show the range of detail and colour available when different, but specific, choices are made.

Note how the choices made in the second interpretation lead to a more compassionate Krogstad and a more assertive Nora.

Alternative 1

UNIT	Krogstad's Unit Objective/*Transitive Verb*	Nora's Unit Objective/*Transitive Verb*
UNIT 1 [Meanwhile there has been a knock at the hall door, but none of them has noticed it. The door is half opened, and	To get Nora to accept that her home and her life are out of her control	To make Krogstad acknowledge that he has broken a boundary by entering uninvited

KROGSTAD appears, he waits a little; the game goes on.]		
KROGSTAD Excuse me, Mrs Helmer.	*Disparage/Unsettle*	
NORA. [With a stifled cry, turns round and gets up on to her knees] Ah! what do you want?		*Repel/Accuse*
KROGSTAD Excuse me, the outer door was ajar; I suppose someone forgot to shut it.	*Patronise/Belittle*	
UNIT 2 NORA. [Rising] My husband is	To make her accept that he is happy to break social rules and is not disturbed by her flustered state	To make him feel uncomfortable and that he should leave

129

out, Mr Krogstad. KROGSTAD I know that.	*Challenge/Disturb*	*Chastise/Scold*
UNIT 3 NORA. What do you want here, then? KROGSTAD A word with you. NORA. With me?—	To make her feel weak and under his control *Intimidate/Unnerve*	To make him accept her authority within her home *Challenge/Dominate* *Implore/Urge*
UNIT 4 [To the children, gently] Go in to nurse. What? No, the strange man won't do mother any harm. When he has gone we will have another game. [She	To get Nora to acknowledge that he has no sympathy for the presence of her children or her role as a mother *Disturb/Unnerve* (Applied without words)	To make the children leave the room without becoming alarmed *Reassure/Calm* (Applied to the children)

takes the children into the room on the left, and shuts the door after them]		
UNIT 5 NORA. You want to speak to me? KROGSTAD. Yes, I do.	To make her feel weak and thereby give in to his demands *Dominate/ Overpower*	To make him acknowledge her vulnerability and show sympathy *Entreat/Soften*
UNIT 6 NORA. Today? It is not the first of the month yet. KROGSTAD. No, it is Christmas Eve, and it will depend on yourself what sort of a Christmas you will spend.	To overwhelm her with a feeling of impending doom *Threaten/Terrify*	To make Krogstad confirm that he has no reason to bother her at this time *Disempower/Dissuade*

131

NORA. What do you mean? Today it is absolutely impossible for me—		Challenge/Implore
KROGSTAD. We won't talk about that until later on.	Control/Taunt	
UNIT 7 KROGSTAD. This is something different. I presume you can give me a moment?	To make her admit that she is keen to know why he needs to speak to her Coerce/Belittle	To make him acknowledge that she still has some power
NORA. Yes—yes, I can— although—		Appease/Subdue
KROGSTAD. Good.	Overpower/Overrule	

Alternative 2

UNIT	Krogstad's Unit Objective/*Transitive Verb*	Nora's Unit Objective/*Transitive Verb*
UNIT 1 [Meanwhile there has been a knock at the hall door, but none of them has noticed it. The door is half opened, and KROGSTAD appears, he waits a little; the game goes on.] KROGSTAD. Excuse me, Mrs Helmer. NORA. [With a stifled cry, turns round and gets up on to her knees] Ah!	To get Nora to accept the legitimacy of his uninvited presence in her home *Entreat/Supplicate*	To make Krogstad acknowledge that he should not have come in

what do you want? KROGSTAD. Excuse me, the outer door was ajar; I suppose someone forgot to shut it.	 *Placate/Appease*	*Reprimand/Chastise*
UNIT 2 NORA. [Rising] My husband is out, Mr Krogstad. KROGSTAD. I know that.	To make Nora accept that she must deal with him alone *Steady/Support*	To make Krogstad confirm that it is not appropriate for him to be alone with her in her home *Correct/Caution*
UNIT 3 NORA. What do you want here, then? KROGSTAD. A word with you. NORA. With me?—	To get Nora to be prepared to engage openly with him *Reassure/Encourage*	To make him confirm that his visit does not concern any threat to her security *Threaten/Intimidate* *Entreat/Supplicate*

UNIT 4 [To the children, gently] Go in to nurse. What? No, the strange man won't do mother any harm. When he has gone we will have another game. [She takes the children into the room on the left, and shuts the door after them]	To get Nora to see and treat him as a reasonable man (i.e. he remains silent and doesn't disturb her relationship with her children) *Respect/Honour* (Applied without words)	To make the children leave the room without becoming alarmed *Coax/Cajole* (Applied to the children)
UNIT 5 NORA. You want to speak to me? KROGSTAD. Yes, I do.	To make her focus on what he says *Focus/Enlist*	To make him accept that she is not afraid of him and thereby stop trying to intimidate her *Confront/Challenge*

UNIT 6		
NORA. Today? It is not the first of the month yet.	To make Nora realise the importance of the forthcoming conversation and to respond accordingly by allowing him to take control	To make Krogstad stop troubling her and leave *Correct/Rebuke*
KROGSTAD. No, it is Christmas Eve, and it will depend on yourself what sort of a Christmas you will spend.		
	Caution/Prepare	
NORA. What do you mean? Today it is absolutely impossible for me—		*Interrogate/Rebuff*
KROGSTAD. We won't talk about that until later on.	*Calm/Appease*	
UNIT 7	To make her listen with an open mind	To make him acknowledge her compromise in allowing the forthcoming conversation
KROGSTAD. This is something different. I	*Entreat/Invite*	

presume you can give me a moment? NORA. Yes—yes, I can—although— KROGSTAD. Good.	*Reward/Congratulate*	*Belittle/Judge*